SYSTAT®

Data

D1511402

DATA

Copyright

References

SYSTAT, Inc.
1800 Sherman Avenue
Evanston, IL 60201-3793
708.**864.5670** Tel.
708.**492.3567** FAX

Contents

Detailed tables of contents for each chapter follow.

Introduction to DATA 1

Entering data 2

Printing data files 3

Saving data in text files 4

Rearranging and combining files 5

Transforming variables 6

Programming in SYSTAT 7

Sorting, ranking, and standardizing 8

Subgroup processing 9

Programming examples 10

MACRO 11

1 Introduction to DATA

Introduction to DATA 1

Overview

SYSTAT has a powerful **DATA** facility for reading and manipulating data. **DATA** is a powerful alternative to the Data Editor and its transformation facilities. **DATA** is a complete programming language. **DATA** has very powerful relational database facilities and **DATA** BASIC, a full-featured implementation of BASIC. Do not explore this volume, however, until you are comfortable with the Data Editor (see the *Getting Started* volume) and have tried some statistical analyses.

Here are some things you can do in either the Editor or with **DATA.**

	Data Editor	*DATA*
Enter data from keyboard	*Type in cell*	*INPUT*
Add cases	*Type in rows*	*APPEND*
Add variables	*Type in columns*	*USE file1 file2*
Drop variables	*DROP*	*DROP*

In general, you should use the Editor for simple or smaller tasks (transformations on a few variables) and consider **DATA** for large tasks (transformations on many variables).

Overview of DATA

The first ten chapters of this volume discuss **DATA.** Chapter 11 is about **MACRO,** which is intended for applications far beyond the capabilities of **DATA.** Here is an overview of the **DATA** chapters:

Entering data (Chapter 2)
You can enter data from the keyboard or read it from plain text (ASCII files). In either case, the data may be either *free-format,* where each value is separated by a comma or a space, or both, or *fixed-format,* where each value appears in the same place in every row (for instance, the first value always starts with the first character of each line, the second value starts on the fifth character, etc.).

Printing data files (Chapter 3)
You can view your data file in its entirety or view and print just certain cases of certain variables.

Saving data in text files (Chapter 4)
You can save data in plain text files suitable for exporting to other applications or platforms. In so doing, you can also change variables from numeric to character, rearrange the file, and reduce the file size.

Rearranging and combining files (Chapter 5)
You can use **DATA** to combine two files side-by-side or one on top of the other. You can rearrange the variables, drop variables, delete cases, and transpose files. You *can* do all of these things (except rearrange variables) with the regular Data Editor, but for large files, **DATA** is more efficient.

Transforming variables (Chapters 6)
DATA allows you to create new variables using a wide range of mathematical functions. Statements like IF...THEN let you do conditional transformations quickly. You can recode variables with a simple CODE statement and add value labels with a LABEL statement. Some of these features are available in the Data Editor, but **DATA** handles a large number of variables more efficiently.

Programming in SYSTAT (Chapter 7)

DATA contains SYSTAT's version of the BASIC (Beginner's All-purpose Symbolic Instruction Code) programming language. BASIC statements like IF...THEN and FOR...NEXT let you do complex transformations quickly.

Sorting, ranking, and standardizing (Chapter 8)

You can sort, rank, and standardize files with the Data Editor, but with **DATA** you can do more complex variations like computing Winsorized and trimmed means, normal scores, medians, etc.

Subgroup processing (Chapter 9)

DATA has four built-in grouping variables: beginning of file, end of file, beginning of group, and end of group. You can use these variables to process your data in subgroups, for example to compute sums, means, medians, etc. within groups.

Programming examples (Chapter 10)

In Chapter 10 we present many examples of more advanced **DATA** applications using principles learned in earlier chapters. Among other things, we show how to do operations across rows in a dataset (for instance, computing means across variables within *cases*) and how to generate various kinds of random data.

Using DATA

Just type **DATA.** This tells SYSTAT that you want to use the **DATA** facilities. Press Return at the end of any **DATA** command, including the DATA command.

Now you're ready to go. Type commands after the prompt (>), one command per prompt, and when you are ready to execute the commands, enter RUN after the prompt. The following chapters will introduce you to the commands. Remember, the commands will not work until you type RUN.

Notation

In the **Command reference** appendices for SYSTAT and **SYGRAPH,** we explain command syntax and notation in great detail. If at any time you are unsure of the notation we use in the command reference sections for **DATA,** just check there.

In the meantime, you only need to know about one convention we use in displaying commands: placeholders. *Placeholders* are words or symbols that we show in *place* of the actual things you would type when using commands.

For example, the first thing you usually do is open a file. The USE command tells **DATA** to open the file you name after the word USE.

```
USE MEDICAL
```

Here, we ask **DATA** to open the file named "MEDICAL." You could name any file after USE.

```
USE BASEBALL
USE US
USE USDATA
```

If you have a file in a different folder, you would give the entire pathname for that file, enclosed in single or double quotation marks:

```
USE 'C:\SYSTAT\DATAFLS\BASEBALL'
USE 'B:MYDATA'
```

You also need to use quotation marks if your filename (or any folder contained in the pathname) contains spaces or symbols. If your file (or any folder named in the path) contains single or double quotation marks, surround the whole thing with the opposite type of marks:

```
USE "Tom's data"
```

As you can see, you could type many different things after USE. Instead of trying to list all the possibilities, we just use the placeholder *filename*:

USE *filename*

Here, *filename* means "any valid filename or pathname, including quotation marks if needed."

You can distinguish placeholders from actual command words because we always print placeholders in *italic, lower-case letters*. Other placeholders you'll see frequently are *varlist*, which means one or more variables, and *n*, which means some number. Usually we give rules, like "*n* can be any positive integer between 1 and 100."

We use square brackets [and] to indicate things that are optional. For instance, you can optionally specify variables for the LIST command:

LIST [*varlist*]

The brackets mean that you can list specific variables if you want, or you can press Return right after the word LIST. Both of the following would be valid commands:

```
LIST
LIST ACCIDENT, CARDIO, CANCER
```

Other abbreviations and notation conventions should become obvious as you study the examples.

HOT and COLD

Finally, you will occasionally see the word HOT in this volume. HOT commands produce output immediately after they are entered. COLD commands, on the other hand, set options or switches. All HOT commands are labeled with the word HOT in the reference lists. The most common HOT command is the RUN command.

2 Entering data

Entering data 2

Overview

This chapter shows you how to create SYSTAT files by typing data from the keyboard and by reading plain text (ASCII) files.

You enter data from the keyboard in the Data Editor. The only reason you might want to use **DATA** would be if you prefer typing spaces to pressing Return between values. For reading ASCII files, unless you require the special control of fixed-format input (see below), you do not need to use **DATA**.

DIAGONAL=<u>PRESENT</u> | ABSENT	Specifies whether the matrix you are entering has values in the diagonal cells. The diagonal is assumed to be present unless you state otherwise with DIAGONAL=ABSENT.
GET *filename*	Reads the ASCII (plain text) file *filename.*
IMPORT *filename* [(*varlist*)]	Translates *filename* into SYSTAT format. You can optionally include *varlist* if you want to import only certain variables from the file.
/ TYPE=DBASE | DBASE2 | DBASE3 | DIF | EXCEL | LOTUS | LOTUS2 | MAP | PORTABLE | SYMPHONY | SYMPHONY11	Specifies importing format. MAP reads map data into .MAP files (see Appendix IV in the *Graphics* volume for information about map files).
RANGE=*rangename*	Specifies the range to import. The default is the entire file.
ROWS=*n1-n2*	Specifies the rows to import. The default is the entire file.
INPUT *varlist*	Names the variables (and indicates order) that will be read into SYSTAT. You may identify a range of variables in *varlist* using subscript notation.
\	For free-format input, place a backslash after *varlist* to force SYSTAT to start a new case for each line of data and to use every value entered in each row, even if it must start filling new cases to do so. See Example 2.8.

INPUT (*varlist*) (*format*).	For fixed-format input, INPUT has two arguments, each enclosed in parentheses. As above, *varlist* indicates the variable names, in order. *Format* is a format description in special notation, discussed in this chapter.
LRECL=*n*	Specifies record length for importing data. *N* is an integer between 0 and 999. You must use LRECL if you are importing data from record longer than 150 columns.
RUN	Executes commands. HOT.
SAVE *filename*	Saves data into the SYSTAT file *filename.*
/'*comment*'	Saves your comments in the file.
DOUBLE | SINGLE	Specifies whether to save in double or single precision.
TYPE = RECTANGULAR | SSCP | COVARIANCE | CORRELATION | DISSIMILARITY | SIMILARITY	Specifies the type of matrix you are entering. Use DIAGONAL=ABSENT if the diagonal values are missing.

DATA provides two basic ways to enter your data into SYSTAT:

1) Read data *from a text* (ASCII) *file*.
2) Type in values *with the keyboard* .

There are three commands that you will always use when creating a SYSTAT file: SAVE, INPUT and RUN. SAVE names the SYSTAT file you are creating. INPUT names the variables you are reading. RUN sets the procedure in motion. In addition, the GET command reads a specified text file.

Keyboard input

```
SAVE filename
INPUT varlist
RUN
```

```
Input data one case at a time after prompt arrow
>
```

File input

```
SAVE filename
INPUT varlist
GET filename
RUN
```

Types of data

SYSTAT accepts numbers and characters as data. Numeric variables contain numbers, and character variables (denoted by a $ at the end of their name) contain character strings.

Numeric values

Numeric values should have no more than 12 digits before or after the decimal point, and a total of no more than 15 digits. You can also separate numeric values with a slash. This allows you to read dates (e.g. 11/5/44) into several variables (e.g. MONTH,DAY,YEAR).

```
13579
.
.326
123456789.
1.9E4
1.9e-4
.8D15
123456789.123456789
```

Scientific notation

Two of the numbers listed above contain the letter E. These numbers are in scientific notation.

$$1.9E4 = 1.9 * 10^4 = 19000$$
$$1.9E\text{-}4 = 1.9 * 10^{-4} = .00019$$

The number containing D works the same way. This is a "double precision" exponent printed by some computer languages. You can use any integer exponent with absolute magnitude less than or equal to 35.

The last example contains 18 decimal digits. Because SYSTAT inputs numbers only up to 15 decimal digits, this number rounds off to 123456789.123457.

Missing numeric values

The period (.) on the second line of our example denotes a missing value. Missing numeric values are set to a number smaller than the smallest value used in any calculations. All the statistical modules recognize this value and exclude it from computations. If you want to denote a missing numeric value when typing from the keyboard or entering data from a file, make sure you use a period. Otherwise, SYSTAT will look for the next value you type and not realize a value was missing.

Numeric variable names

Numeric variable names are 1 to 8 letters and/or numbers beginning with a letter. They may be subscripted. Some valid numeric variable names are:

```
POPDEN    TEST(1)       MAGNITUD      POPULATN
```

Character values

Character variables may contain strings up to 12 characters long. They should be separated by blanks and/or commas and may be surrounded by quotation marks (' or "). The values *must* be surrounded by quotation marks if they contain embedded blanks and/or special characters. If more than 12 characters exist in the input value, the value is truncated to the first 12. If fewer than 12 characters exist, blanks are inserted at the end. Here are some examples:

```
MALE
'New York'
ANTIDISESTABLISHMENTARIANISM
```

The last string in this example is truncated to ANTIDISESTAB when it is stored. If there are more variables to be read from the line, SYSTAT begins with LISHMENTARIANISM. This causes an error when **DATA** is expecting a numeric value. If the next variable to be read is a character variable, you get no error message—you just get a messed up data file. Be careful.

Missing character values

Missing values for character variables are denoted with a blank surrounded by quotation marks: (" ") or (' ')

Character variable names

Remember to use dollar signs with character variable names. If you try to read character data into a numeric variable, SYSTAT prints an error message and lists the data it was unable to process. Some valid names for character variables are:

```
NAME$       REGION$        HOMETOWN$      X$
```

Free- and fixed-format input

There are two types of input. *Free-format input* works with delimited data (data where each value is separated by spaces or commas), and *fixed-format input* works with data where the values of variables are in the same locations in each record. Each is discussed in more detail below.

Record length

If you are importing data from records longer than 150 columns, you must use the LRECL command. Its syntax is:

```
LRECL=n
```

where *n* is an integer between 0 and 999, inclusive. The default is 150.

Importing files from other applications

The IMPORT command allows you to translate files from other formats directly into SYSTAT files. See the *Getting Started* manual for more information.

Free-format input

After seeing a RUN command, SYSTAT looks for data values. If you typed GET before RUN, SYSTAT looks for the file you named and reads the data values from it. Otherwise, SYSTAT expects you to type the values from the keyboard.

Whether typed from the keyboard or read from a file, data values must be separated by tabs, commas, or spaces. Each new case should begin on a separate line (press the Return key to start a new line). You may read several lines of values into a single case, but each case must begin on a new line.

Character values that contain blanks, commas, or special characters must be surrounded by single or double quotation marks (' or "). Missing values must be represented by a period (.) for numeric variables or a blank surrounded by quotation marks (" " or ' ') for character variables.

SYSTAT continues reading the data until it encounters the end of a file, a tilde (~) sign or, if it is expecting numeric data, a non-numeric string. In general, this means that you can end a batch of numeric data by typing another command. When in doubt, use a tilde to end the input explicitly.

To read data from a text file, add a GET *filename* command before the run command. GET tells SYSTAT that the data you want to read is located in an ASCII file. The file must be plain ASCII text, containing no page breaks, margin indicators, or control characters. It must contain only raw data, with no column headings or variable labels.

2.1 Keyboard input

Create a small SYSTAT file by entering the following commands in **DATA:**

```
SAVE MYFILE
INPUT A B C
RUN
```

```
Input data one case at a time after prompt arrow
>
```

Now enter data one case to a line:

```
1 2 3
4 5 6
7 8 9
~
```

The last character is a tilde that tells SYSTAT to end data input. SYSTAT responds:

```
    3 cases and     3 variables processed.
SYSTAT file created
```

You have just entered data from the keyboard and saved it to a SYSTAT data file named MYFILE

2.2 Reading from a text file

The procedure is similar for reading data from a text file. Suppose the data you typed in above is in a text file called INFILE. To import it, you would enter these commands:

```
GET INFILE
SAVE MYFILE
INPUT A B C
RUN
```

```
    3 cases and     3 variables processed.
SYSTAT file created.
```

The only difference between this and the first example is that you use the GET command to tell SYSTAT that the data is coming from a text file.

The ASCII file must not contain nonprinting ASCII characters. There must be no page breaks, control characters, column markers, margin indicators, etc. SYSTAT *can* read numbers, alphabetic and keyboard characters, delimiters (spaces, commas, or slashes that separate consecutive values from each other), and carriage returns.

2.3 Unequal length records

For each new case, SYSTAT reads as many data values as are named in the INPUT command, one value per variable. This example shows what happens when each input record has a different number of data values. Enter the following commands in **DATA**:

```
NEW
SAVE MYFILE
INPUT A B C D
RUN
```

```
Input data one case at a time after prompt arrow
>
```

Now enter the following data, separating the values with spaces:

```
10 20 30 40
50 60
70 80
90 100 110 120
~
```

```
    3 cases and    4 variables processed
SYSTAT file created.
```

To view the contents of this new SYSTAT file, type:

```
LIST
RUN
```

```
                         A          B          C          D

 Case     1         10.000     20.000     30.000     40.000
 Case     2         50.000     60.000     70.000     80.000
 Case     3         90.000    100.000    110.000    120.000

    3 cases and    4 variables processed
No SYSTAT file created.
```

Line by line, here is what SYSTAT does:

Case 1. SYSTAT reads the four data points from the first record of original data into the first case of the SYSTAT file.

Case 2. SYSTAT now reads the two data points from the second record (50 and 60) into variables A and B, respectively, in case 2 of the SYSTAT file.

SYSTAT must still fill variables C and D for case 2. It therefore reads the data points 70 and 80 from the third record of original data into C and D in the second case of the SYSTAT file.

Case 3. SYSTAT now begins a new case in the SYSTAT file and so proceeds to the next record of original data. It reads the four data points 90, 100, 110, and 120 into case 3 of the SYSTAT file.

This example would work the same way if you entered these data from a file.

2.4
Records with extraneous data values

For each new case, SYSTAT begins on a new line to read as many data values as are named in the INPUT command. This example demonstrates what happens for a case when there are more values left on a record than needed to fill variables named in the INPUT command.

```
NEW
SAVE NEWFILE
INPUT A B C D
RUN
```

At the subsequent prompt, enter the following records of data:

```
10 20 30
40 50 60 70 80
90 100 110 120 130 140
~
```

```
    2 cases and    4 variables processed
SYSTAT file created.
```

Note that SYSTAT processed the *three* records into *two* cases. List the file:

```
LIST
RUN

                         A          B          C          D

Case      1          10.000     20.000     30.000     40.000
Case      2          90.000    100.000    110.000    120.000

   2 cases and    4 variables processed
No SYSTAT file created.
```

What has happened to the original data? SYSTAT did not read the values 50, 60, 70, 80, or 130 and 140 into the SYSTAT file.

Case 1. SYSTAT reads the values 10, 20, and 30 from the first record of original data into variables A, B, and C, respectively. SYSTAT still needs a value for D in case 1, so it takes the value 40 from the second record of data and puts it there.

Case 2. SYSTAT now starts a new case (case 2) in the SYSTAT file. It assumes that a new case in the SYSTAT file corresponds with a new record of original data, so it jumps down to the third line of data, thereby skipping the numbers 50, 60, 70, and 80.

The value 90 becomes the first number for case 2 of the SYSTAT file. SYSTAT reads the next three data points from record three of original data into variables B, C, and D. Since SYSTAT has completed the case, it never reads the numbers 130 and 140.

2.5 Incorrect treatment of missing values

SYSTAT represents missing numeric data as a period. (Internally, SYSTAT codes missing values as the smallest possible negative value.) It treats missing character data as blanks.

Code missing *numeric* data as periods in your original data. You cannot code missing numeric data as a character value such as NA, M, *, or ? because SYSTAT will not read character data into a numeric field. Also, if missing numbers are left as blank spaces in your original data, SYSTAT reads the blank space as a delimiter. It places the next value in the file where the missing value should be, and all subsequent data are displaced (see example below).

Code missing *character* data as a blank space enclosed in single or double quotation marks, e.g. " ". Do not merely leave values blank.

The following example demonstrates what happens when you do not code missing values as periods.

```
SAVE NEWFILE
INPUT A, B, C
RUN
```

Enter these data:

```
100 200 300
400     600
700 800 900
```

SYSTAT produces the following incorrect file:

```
              A              B              C

Case 1     100.000        200.000        300.000
Case 2     400.000        600.000        700.000
```

Instead of three cases, SYSTAT produces two, skipping over the values 800 and 900. This is similar to Example 2.4. SYSTAT reads the first line of data correctly, but treats the missing value in the second line as a space delimiter separating the values 400 and 600. SYSTAT therefore places 600 under variable B in the case 2 of the SYSTAT file. It completes case 2 by reading 700, the first value of the next line of raw data. Now, since SYSTAT starts a new case in the SYSTAT file, it jumps to the next line of original data. There are no more lines of data to read in, however, so SYSTAT closes the file.

You *could* read these data with fixed-format input (see below). The next example, however, shows how to do it successfully with free-format input.

2.6 Correct treatment of missing values

If we correctly code the missing data point as a period in our original data:

```
100 200 300
400  .  600
700 800 900
```

SYSTAT produces the following correct SYSTAT file:

```
                          A          B          C

Case    1           100.000    200.000    300.000
Case    2           400.000       .       600.000
Case    3           700.000    800.000    900.000
```

SYSTAT reads the data into the appropriate columns and cases and codes the missing value as a period. If the missing data value had been in a character variable, then we would have used a quoted blank (" ") instead.

2.7 Multiple cases per record: backslash

If you want to read more than one case per line, append the backslash (\) to your INPUT statement. The backslash forces SYSTAT to use all the data in every row, even if it has to start filling a new case to finish using the row of values. Also, the backslash forces SYSTAT to start a new case whenever it starts reading a new row of values.

Recall that, without a backslash, SYSTAT skips over any extra values in a row, and it fills every case, even if it has to read several lines of data to do so.

In other words, the backslash forces SYSTAT to use all of the values you enter and to pay attention to your line breaks.

This example shows how to use the backslash to read data where you have more than one case per line of original data.

```
NEW
SAVE MULTIPLE
INPUT NAME$, AGE \
RUN

TOM 23 JERRY 51 MARILYN 50 LYNNE 18
MARK 22 ANDREW 8 HENRY 70 CHRIS 23
~
```

```
    8 cases and     2 variables processed
SYSTAT file created.
```

Display the file you have just created.

```
LIST
RUN
```

```
                          NAME$          AGE

Case       1                TOM        23.000
Case       2              JERRY        51.000
Case       3            MARILYN        50.000
Case       4              LYNNE        18.000
Case       5               MARK        22.000
Case       6             ANDREW         8.000
Case       7              HENRY        70.000
Case       8              CHRIS        23.000

    8 cases and     2 variables processed
No SYSTAT file created.
```

This input works because we used the backslash. SYSTAT reads the entire line of original data even though each line fills up four cases in the SYSTAT file. Without the backslash, SYSTAT would have read only the first two values from each line of data, producing the following file:

```
                          NAME$          AGE

Case       1                TOM        23.000
Case       2               MARK        22.000
```

2.8 Incomplete records: backslash

The following example shows how to use the backslash to read records that do not have an equal number of values per case.

```
NEW
SAVE UNEQUAL
INPUT A B C D\
RUN

1 2 3
4 5 6 7
8 9
~

    3 cases and    4 variables processed
SYSTAT file created.
```

The SYSTAT data file looks like this:

		A	B	C	D
Case	1	1.000	2.000	3.000	.
Case	2	4.000	5.000	6.000	7.000
Case	3	8.000	9.000	.	.

2.9 Incorrect use of backslash

The following example shows how to use the backslash to read records that do not have an equal number of values per line.

```
NEW
SAVE KLUDGE
INPUT A B C \
RUN

1 2 3 4 5
6 7
8
~

    4 cases and    3 variables processed
SYSTAT file created.
```

The SYSTAT data file looks like this:

		A	B	C
Case	1	1.000	2.000	3.000
Case	2	4.000	5.000	.
Case	3	6.000	7.000	.
Case	4	8.000	.	.

Here is how SYSTAT read the data:

Case 1. SYSTAT reads the first three values from the first line of original data (1, 2, and 3) into the first case of the SYSTAT file.

Case 2. SYSTAT begins a new case in the SYSTAT file. With the backslash appended to our INPUT command, SYSTAT does not jump to a new line of original data. Rather, it stays on the same input record and reads the remaining values (4 and 5) into variables A and B of case 2.

These values fill only the first two columns in case 2 of the SYSTAT file. Without the backslash, SYSTAT would complete the case with the first value from the next line of original data. The backslash, however, causes SYSTAT to fill the remaining values for the case with missing values.

Case 3. SYSTAT begins case 3 of the SYSTAT file, reading data from the next line of original data (line 2). It reads two values from this line (6 and 7) into the first two variables, and assigns a missing value to the third variable.

Case 4. SYSTAT begins case 4 of the SYSTAT file and reads the data from the next line of original data (line 3). It reads the first and only value from this line (8) and fills the remaining two cells with missing values.

If we had not used the backslash in the INPUT statement, SYSTAT would have produced the following file:

		A	B	C
Case	1	1.000	2.000	3.000
Case	2	6.000	7.000	8.000

SYSTAT fills the first case with the values 1, 2, and 3. The case complete, it starts a second and begins reading from the second input line. Thus, the values 4 and 5 are lost. SYSTAT puts the values 6 and 7 in case 2 under variables A and B, and reads the third value for this case from the third line of data.

Fixed-format input

With fixed-format input, you tell SYSTAT exactly where the values for each variable are located in the data records. Values for a variable must be in the same place for every record.

There are two parts to a fixed-format input statement. In the first part, name the variables as you want them to appear in the SYSTAT file. The second part of the statement contains the format, which determines where SYSTAT reads values for each variable.

As usual, variable names must be 8 characters or less. Be sure to use dollar signs to indicate character variables. The data type of a format item (character or numeric) must match the data type of its respective variable name. Finally, the number of items specified in the format must match the number of input variables.

Enclose the variable names and the input format in separate sets of parentheses, like this:

```
INPUT (AGE,SEX$,INCOME) (#3,$6,#8)
```

The format controls a pointer that tells SYSTAT where to read the next variable value. SYSTAT checks the number of items you specify in the format against the number of variables. If they do not match, it is an error.

Formats

Formats specify the location and width of fields that contain values. Leading and trailing blanks are ignored for numeric data. All characters within the formatted field, except leading blanks, are read into a character value. In other words, character strings are left-justified.

Format items for fixed-format input include the following:

#*n*	reads a numeric variable in the next *n* columns
$*n*	reads a character variable in the next *n* columns
>	moves the pointer one column to the right
<	moves the pointer one column to the left
^*n*	moves the pointer to column *n*
/	moves the pointer to the first column on the next record
%*n*	moves the pointer to the first column on the *n*th record
****	leaves the pointer on the current record for next case
n*r	repeats *r n* times, where *r* is any of the above

Some examples:

>>>	moves the pointer 3 columns to the right
3*>	moves the pointer 3 columns to the right
^10	moves to column 10 of the current record
#4	reads the numeric value in the next 4 columns beginning at the column where the pointer is now
$5	reads the character value in the next 5 columns beginning at the column where the pointer is now
^3	moves the pointer to column 3
>>>>>	moves the pointer 5 columns beyond its current position.
5*>	does the same thing
%2	moves the pointer to column 1 of the second record (You may not skip back to an earlier record)
/	moves the pointer to column 1 of the next record
//	moves the pointer to column 1 two records ahead. (Thus, if you are starting on the first record, %3 and // mean the same thing)
#3	reads the numeric value in the 3 columns beginning at the current pointer position
2*$3	reads a character value in three columns and then another in the next three columns

Note that \ does not skip to the next record before reading a new case. This feature is useful for reading files with different numbers of records per case.

It is generally safer to use % and ^ rather than / and >, since the former ensure that you know precisely which record and column you are on. Furthermore, if you have 7 records per observation, you need a %7 at the end of your format, even if you read nothing from the seventh field, to insure that the pointer is positioned correctly for the next observation.

Here is a simple example for reading some data with a format.

```
INPUT (A,B$,C) (#3 $5 > #3)
RUN
120abcde 007
121fghij 999
~
```

The tilde (~) indicates that you will not enter any more data.

Note: if your INPUT statement takes up more than one line, do not let the statement wrap around to the next line. Rather, end the first line with a comma, press Enter, and keep typing the statement on the next line. Do this for as many lines as you need.

2.10
Simple example

Suppose you have an ASCII file TESTDATA like the following. The two italicized lines are to help you count columns.

```
0        1         2
12345678901234567890123456
1232 BILLY 0 1 1 1 0 BACDD
BCEAD
7384 SUSAN 1 1 0 1 1 BDAEA
DDEAE
2837   TIM 1 1 1 0 1 CBADE
DDBCA
7484   TOM 0 0 1 0 1 BCDEC
AAEDC
5678 WAYNE 1 1 0 1 0 ADEAA
DACBB
```

The first variable in the file is a four-column ID number. The second is the first name of a student. The next five variables are answers to true-false questions and are separated by spaces. The last five variables on the first line are answers to multiple-choice questions and are not delimited. The variables on the second line are answers to five more multiple choice questions.

SYSTAT reads the data into a SYSTAT file called TEST.SYS. Because the INPUT statement takes up more than one line, we use commas to continue it onto subsequent lines.

```
GET TESTDATA
SAVE TEST
INPUT (ID,NAME$,Q(1-5),Q6$,Q7$,Q8$,Q9$,Q10$,
        Q11$,Q12$,Q13$,Q14$,Q15$),
      (#4,$6,5*#2,>,5*$1,%2,5*$1)
RUN
```

Here is how each variable is read by its format description:

#4 Reads numeric value from first four columns into variable ID.
$6 Reads character value from next six columns into NAME$.
5*#2 Reads five consecutive two-column numeric values into Q(1), Q(2), Q(3), Q(4), and Q(5).
> Moves pointer one space to the right.
5*$1 Reads five consecutive one-column character values into Q6$, Q7$, Q8$, Q9$, and Q10$.
%2 Moves pointer to second line of input record.
5*$1 Reads five consecutive one-column character values into Q11$, Q12$, Q13$, Q14$, and Q15$.

Entering triangular matrices

Data in SYSTAT files assume cases-by-rows (rectangular) form by default. Both **DATA** and the regular Data Editor allow you to enter triangular matrices, such as might be produced by **CORR**. (See the *Getting Started* manual for instruction on how to do this with the Data Editor.)

TYPE

Use the TYPE command to indicate what type of matrix you are entering. The default is RECTANGULAR. SSCP designates a sum of squares and cross products matrix. COVARIANCE designates a covariance matrix. CORRELATION designates a correlation matrix. DISSIMILARITY and SIMILARITY indicate dissimilarity and similarity data, respectively. Some procedures like **CORR** and **MDS** output a triangular matrix to a SYSTAT file and automatically set the type.

If you LIST a triangular matrix in **DATA**, the upper triangular portion is missing values, since the matrices are symmetric and only half of the values are needed by the statistical routines.

2.11
Entering a covariance matrix

Here is an example of how to enter a covariance matrix and save it in a file named TURTLE.

```
SAVE TURTLE
INPUT LENGTH,WIDTH,HEIGHT
TYPE COVARIANCE
RUN
451.39
271.17 171.73
168.70 103.29 66.65
~
```

2.12 Entering a matrix with missing diagonal

For some types of data, the values on the diagonal are undefined or constant. You may, in these cases, input only the values below the diagonal and leave the diagonal missing. Use DIAGONAL ABSENT to signal to **DATA** that the diagonal values are missing.

If you do not use the command, DIAGONAL PRESENT is assumed. If you input a correlation matrix with DIAGONAL ABSENT, SYSTAT sets the diagonal elements to 1.0. Otherwise, the diagonal elements are set to missing values.

Here is an example of how to input a similarity matrix with the diagonal elements omitted.

```
SAVE COLORS
INPUT RED,ORANGE,YELLOW,GREEN,BLUE,INDIGO,VIOLET
TYPE SIMILARITY
DIAGONAL ABSENT
RUN
10
 9  9
 7 10 10
 1  4  9 10
 6  5  7  9  9
 9  8  5  8  9 10
~
```

Notice that there are only 6 rows and columns to fill 7 variables. The diagonal elements are set to missing. The example above saves data in a SYSTAT file named COLORS for possible use by the multidimensional scaling procedure **MDS**.

Trouble-shooting

The previous examples apply also to ASCII file input; the same sorts of mistakes that one can make when entering data from the keyboard will also cause input from ASCII files to be interpreted incorrectly.

You also must be sure that your ASCII file does not contain any "funny," i.e. nonprinting, ASCII characters. The file can contain no page breaks, control characters, column markers, etc. SYSTAT can read numbers, alphabetic and keyboard characters, delimiters (spaces, commas, or slashes that separate consecutive values from each other), and carriage returns. SYSTAT does its best to interpret other characters but makes no guarantees.

Also, *numeric fields must contain only numeric data*. Therefore, exclude variable labels or column headings from the ASCII file.

You can use a word processor to examine ASCII files. If you see anything in the file other than numbers or typewriter characters, or if the cursor jumps around erratically on the screen, you do not have an ASCII file that SYSTAT can read. Some editors such as Microsoft Word and Word Perfect can display hidden markers (tabs, carriage returns, column markers, page breaks, etc.) so that you can remove them.

Errors and error messages

Following are some of the error messages encountered when reading ASCII files.

Empty file error

```
Error: you are trying to read an empty or nonexistent file
```

Make sure you spelled the file name correctly.

Make sure the file is in the current folder. If it is not, either copy it to the current folder or specify the fully-qualified file name (path plus full file name) in quotes.

Make sure the file is a plain text file (ASCII text, non-document, etc.), not some other format.

Long INPUT statement

If your INPUT statement is too long for one line, end the first line with a comma and press Enter before the line wraps around on your screen (before column 80). Continue typing the statement on the next line. Do this for as many lines as you need.

Data lost or in the wrong columns

If SYSTAT places data incorrectly or data is lost when you read it, check the following:

Make sure you correctly specify missing values in your data file. If you are using free-format input, enter missing numeric values as periods (.) and missing character values as blanks surrounded by quotation marks (" "). If you are using fixed-format input, you may leave missing values as blank spaces.

If you are using free-format input to read a file that does not have the same number of values in every record, add the backslash (\) to the end of your INPUT statement (see above).

Unexpected data error

```
Error:  unexpected data for case   #   at end of this line:
last data entered before error was encountered
This may result from character data in numeric field or vice versa
```

Make sure the ASCII file includes no field headings or variable labels.

Make sure variable types match data types. Do not put character data under a numeric variable or vice-versa.

Make sure you correctly specify missing values. With free-format input, put a period where there are missing numbers. In fixed-format input, you may leave missing values as blank spaces.

If you are using free-format input to read a file that does not have the same number of values in every record, add the backslash (\) to the end of your INPUT statement.

If you are using fixed-format input, make sure you specify the variable types in the format section correctly (*$n* for character data, *#n* for numeric). Also, make sure the format correctly tells SYSTAT where the values for each variable are located.

Non-ASCII character warning

If you try to read an ASCII file and receive the warning

```
***Warning*** Non-ASCII character on case   #   will be converted
to blank
```

check for non-printing characters in your file. Such characters include control characters, tab markers, margin and page-break indicators, etc.

Nonmatching number of variables error

If, with fixed-format input, you receive the error message

```
Error: number of format items does not match number of variables
```

the number of variables defined in the format of your INPUT statement does not match the number of variables named in the variable list.

Input past end of record error

If, with fixed-format input, you receive the error message

```
Error: input past end of record. Check your format.
```

the format of your INPUT statement tells SYSTAT to read out along your ASCII file records further than allowed. This message should rarely occur.

3 Printing data files

Printing data files 3

Overview

The simplest tasks in SYSTAT's **DATA** facilities are viewing and printing files. You can accomplish both tasks quite easily using the regular Data Editor (see the *Getting Started* manual), but the tasks introduce you to some basic **DATA** commands that you will need for more complicated tasks.

Command reference

LIST [*varlist*]	Lists the contents of the file named by the USE statement. *Varlist* is an optional list of variables for viewing a portion of the file only .
OUTPUT * | @ | *filename*	Redirects output. Use * to send output to the screen (the default), @ to send to the printer, or specify a filename to save to a file.
PRINT *varlist* | '*string*'	Displays the values of the variables listed in *varlist*, or displays the character string you specify surrounded by quotes. *Varlist* may include numeric or character variables. See Chapter 7 for information on using the character string argument.
REPEAT *n*	Applies subsequent commands to the first *n* cases in the file. If you type REPEAT without specifying a number, *n*=0 is assumed.
RUN	Sets a **DATA** procedure in motion. HOT.
USE *filename* [(*varlist*)]	Retrieves the SYSTAT data file *filename*. *Varlist* is an optional list of variables that you can use if you only want to work with some of the variables in *filename*.

Printing data

LIST

Use the LIST command to view a file as follows:

```
USE filename
LIST [varlist]
RUN
```

When you open a SYSTAT file with the USE command, SYSTAT displays the names of all the variables in the file. You can then specify the variables you want to see with LIST. If you do not specify any variables, SYSTAT lists the contents of all the variables in the file. Type RUN to have SYSTAT perform the commands you have specified.

SYSTAT shows all the cases of the variables. If you only want to see some of the cases, you can specify a number of cases with REPEAT.

```
REPEAT n
```

When you want to list more than 5 variables, you may want to add:

```
PAGE=WIDE
```

This way, SYSTAT prints 9 variables per line. See Appendix I, **DATA command reference**, for further information.

You can control the number of decimal places to be printed with the FORMAT command. See Appendix I, **DATA command reference**, for further information.

3.1 Listing the first ten cases

To list the first ten cases of the variables SPIRITS, WINE, and BEER from the SYSTAT file USDATA, enter:

```
USE USDATA
```

SYSTAT responds by listing the variables in the file:

```
SYSTAT file variables available to you are:
     STATE$         REGION$         REGION       DIVISION$      DIVISION
   LANDAREA           POP85       ACCIDENT         CARDIO         CANCER
   PULMONAR        PNEU_FLU       DIABETES          LIVER        DOCTORS
   HOSPITAL        MARRIAGE        DIVORCE       FDSTAMPS       TEACHERS
    TCHRSAL          HSGRAD         AVGPAY       TOTALSLE       BLDGMTRL
    MRCHDSE        FOODSTRS       AUTODLRS       GASSTATN        APPAREL
   FURNITUR        EATNDRNK       DRUGSTRE       ALLSALES        VIOLENT
   VIOLRATE        PROPERTY       PROPRATE       PRISONER        SPIRITS
       WINE            BEER          TAXES
```

Now use REPEAT to specify ten cases, LIST to name the three variables you want to see, and RUN to start:

```
REPEAT 10
LIST SPIRITS, WINE, BEER
RUN
```

```
                      SPIRITS         WINE         BEER

 Case     1             2.680        2.710       30.160
 Case     2             6.180        5.000       48.100
 Case     3             3.040        4.120       35.660
 Case     4             3.210        4.250       31.890
 Case     5             2.700        4.370       32.820
 Case     6             3.170        4.180       26.580
 Case     7             2.720        4.140       27.580
 Case     8             2.900        4.600       28.610
 Case     9             1.740        1.840       33.010
 Case    10             1.600        2.090       33.980

   10 cases and    43 variables processed.
 No SYSTAT file created.
```

3.2 Listing many variables

If you LIST more variables than SYSTAT can fit on one line, the cases continue or "wrap around" on subsequent lines. For example, the following LIST command does not specify any variables. Therefore, SYSTAT lists all the variables in the file.

```
REPEAT 3
LIST
RUN
```

The first three cases of USDATA look like this:

```
                          STATE$       REGION$       REGION    DIVISION$   DIVISION
                        LANDAREA         POP85     ACCIDENT       CARDIO     CANCER
                        PULMONAR      PNEU_FLU     DIABETES        LIVER    DOCTORS
                        HOSPITAL      MARRIAGE      DIVORCE     FDSTAMPS   TEACHERS
                         TCHRSAL        HSGRAD       AVGPAY     TOTALSLE   BLDGMTRL
                         MRCHDSE      FOODSTRS     AUTODLRS     GASSTATN    APPAREL
                        FURNITUR      EATNDRNK     DRUGSTRE     ALLSALES    VIOLENT
                        VIOLRATE      PROPERTY     PROPRATE     PRISONER    SPIRITS
                            WINE          BEER        TAXES

Case     1                    ME     Northeast        1.000 New England       1.000
Case     1             33265.000      1164.000       37.700      466.200    213.800
Case     1                33.600        21.100       15.600       14.500   1773.000
Case     1                47.000        12.600        5.900      120.000     12.300
Case     1             17328.000        14.600    14130.000     5169.000    304.000
Case     1               462.000      1275.000      914.000      387.000    210.000
Case     1               133.000       411.000      161.000     5332.000      1.800
Case     1               160.000        40.400     3522.000     1025.000      2.680
Case     1                 2.710        30.160        0.630
Case     2                    NH     Northeast        1.000 New England       1.000
Case     2              9279.000       998.000       35.900      395.900    182.200
Case     2                29.600        20.100       17.600       10.400   1612.000
Case     2                34.000        11.100        4.600       41.000      9.700
Case     2             17376.000        11.500    15541.000     5239.000    332.000
Case     2               525.000      1252.000      949.000      398.000    244.000
Case     2               192.000       418.000      133.000     5354.000      1.200
Case     2               125.000        31.000     3231.000      527.000      6.180
Case     2                 5.000        48.100        1.030
Case     3                    VT     Northeast        1.000 New England       1.000
Case     3              9614.000       535.000       41.300      433.100    188.100
Case     3                33.100        24.000       15.600       13.100   1154.000
Case     3                19.000         5.500        2.500       50.000      6.200
Case     3             17931.000         6.000    14643.000     2529.000    173.000
Case     3               171.000       596.000      464.000      217.000    107.000
Case     3                76.000       217.000       68.000     2601.000      0.700
Case     3               133.000        21.000     4000.000      536.000      3.040
Case     3                 4.120        35.660        0.450

    3 cases and   43 variables processed.
No SYSTAT file created.
```

The individual cases are too long to fit on one line, so each case occupies nine lines. Consider PAGE=WIDE to list 9 variables on a line instead of 5.

PRINT

The PRINT command prints values of variables you specify. It is similar to LIST, except case numbers and variable names are not printed. Examples:

```
PRINT AGE, SEX$
PRINT A, B, C, NAME$
```

If you do not include an argument after PRINT, a blank line is printed.

3.3
Printing several variables

Compare the following with the output produced in Example 3.1. Notice how the variable names and case numbers are missing. With PAGE=WIDE, you can display up to 10 variables on a line.

```
USE USDATA
REPEAT 3
PRINT SPIRITS, WINE, BEER
RUN
```

```
        2.680       2.710      30.160
        6.180       5.000      48.100
        3.040       4.120      35.660
```

SYSTAT prints numeric and character values in 12-column, right-justified fields. Blanks pad the left side of each field. You can use FORMAT to set the number of decimal places shown for numeric values.

OUTPUT

To obtain a hard copy from your printer, include the OUTPUT @ command with LIST or PRINT.

The command OUTPUT * redirects output back to the screen when your computer is done printing the SYSTAT file.

3.4
Printing three cases

This example prints the first three cases of USDATA.

```
USE USDATA
OUTPUT @
REPEAT 3
LIST
RUN
OUTPUT *
```

When you type RUN, SYSTAT sends the same output shown in the previous example to your printer while also displaying it on your screen. Notice that OUTPUT * is used at the end to redirect output to the screen.

4 Saving data in text files

Saving data in text files 4

Overview

This chapter shows how to convert SYSTAT data files to plain text files in various formats.

OUTPUT * | @ | *filename*	Redirects output. Use * to send output to the screen (the default), @ to send to the printer, or specify a filename to save to a file.
PUT *filename*	Saves data in a SYSTAT data file into a plain text (ASCII) file with comma delimiters.

USE and PUT

The general strategy is to open a SYSTAT data file with USE, specify an output ASCII file with PUT, and then type RUN.

```
USE datafile
PUT outputfile
RUN
```

PUT saves your data in a text file that has up to 12 columns, with each column separated by commas. Character values (strings) are surrounded by double quotation marks (").

Decimal places

Numeric values default to 3 decimal places. You can change this by placing a FORMAT command before RUN. For example, this program will write 7 digits after the decimal:

```
USE datafile
PUT outputfile
FORMAT=7
RUN
```

OUTPUT and PRINT

You can also use OUTPUT and PRINT to save data to an ASCII file: OUTPUT redirects PRINT so that it saves the values of the variables you specify in a file, rather than displaying them on the screen.

```
USE datafile
PRINT varlist
OUTPUT outputfile
RUN
```

Varlist specifies the variable(s) you want to include in the ASCII file. After you are done, remember to direct output back to the screen again with OUTPUT *.

4.1 Putting data into a text file

The following commands convert the SYSTAT file USDATA to a text file .

```
USE USDATA
PUT TEXTFILE
RUN
```

You can use a word processor to view TEXTFILE. The first case in the file appears as follows:

```
"ME          ","Northeast   ",      1.000,"New England ",
1.000,   33265.000,    1164.000,      37.700,      466.200,
213.800,      33.600,      21.100,      15.600,      14.500,
1773.000,      47.000,      12.600,       5.900,     120.000,
12.300,   17328.000,      14.600,   14130.000,    5169.000,
304.000,     462.000,    1275.000,     914.000,     387.000,
210.000,     133.000,     411.000,     161.000,    5332.000,
1.800,     160.000,      40.400,    3522.000,    1025.000,
2.680,       2.710,      30.160,       0.630
```

This is one record, with a carriage return appearing only at the end. The record “wraps around” here for display purposes. Notice that commas are used as data separators and character variables are surrounded by quotes. This is not true if you use PRINT, as in the following examples.

4.2 Saving selected cases

You can save only certain cases in a text file by using IF ... THEN PRINT. Here is an example:

```
USE USDATA
OUTPUT TEXTFILE
IF REGION$="Northeast" THEN PRINT BEER WINE
RUN
OUTPUT *
```

Other possible selections are statements like:

```
IF CASE=1 OR CASE=3 OR CASE=34 THEN PRINT BEER WINE
IF SPIRITS>2 AND SPIRITS<3 THEN PRINT BEER WINE
```

4.3 Saving selected variables

You can save only certain variables in a text file by listing variable names in the USE command.

```
USE USDATA (REGION DIVISION BEER WINE)
PUT TEXTFILE
RUN
```

4.4 Changing a variable's type

To change a character variable to a numeric variable or vice versa, you must create a new variable of the correct type. You cannot do this with the Data Editor. If the numeric variable you want to change has few values, use SYSTAT transformation statements to create the new variable. You can most efficiently create a character variable from a categorical numeric variable with the LABEL command.

If the variable has many values, however, create a text file containing the variable you want to change by using OUTPUT and PRINT. Then, read the variable back into the original file in the desired format using the GET and INPUT commands. Then you can drop the original variable from the file, if you wish.

This example uses the variables BEER, SPIRITS, and WINE from USDATA. It outputs the values of BEER to a text file and then reads those values back into the character variable BEER$. Thus, it changes a numeric to a character variable. The results are saved in the file FINAL.

This first step creates the text file TEXT. The command OUTPUT TEXT directs subsequent output to the file TEXT. The OUTPUT * command causes SYSTAT to close TEXT and redirect output to the screen.

```
USE USDATA
OUTPUT TEXT
PRINT BEER
RUN

OUTPUT *
```

This step reads the variables SPIRITS, WINE, and BEER from USDATA, drops the variable BEER, reads the values from TEXT into BEER$, and saves the results in the file FINAL.

```
USE USDATA(SPIRITS WINE BEER)
SAVE FINAL
GET TEXT
INPUT BEER$
DROP BEER
RUN
```

A listing of the first ten cases of FINAL produces:

```
                    SPIRITS        WINE       BEER$

 Case      1          2.680       2.710      30.160
 Case      2          6.180       5.000      48.100
 Case      3          3.040       4.120      35.660
 Case      4          3.210       4.250      31.890
 Case      5          2.700       4.370      32.820
 Case      6          3.170       4.180      26.580
 Case      7          2.720       4.140      27.580
 Case      8          2.900       4.600      28.610
 Case      9          1.740       1.840      33.010
 Case     10          1.600       2.090      33.980
```

Do not confuse the values in the variable BEER$ with numeric values. They are now *numerals*, not numbers, which can be used to label cases as discrete categories. If you try to compute statistics or transformations on BEER$, you will get an error message.

4.5 Unpacking records

This example shows how to transform several repeated measures on a single record into one measure per record. We use subscripted variable names for convenience.

```
SAVE TRIAL
INPUT X(1-5), SEX$
RUN

10 20 30 40 50 Male
11 21 31 41 51 Female
~
```

The file contains two records:

```
                 X(1)          X(2)          X(3)          X(4)          X(5)
SEX$

 Case 1      10.000        20.000        30.000        40.000        50.000
Male
 Case 2      11.000        21.000        31.000        41.000        51.000
Female
```

The following commands make a new file with 10 records. First, create a temporary text file with 10 records, each containing one data value plus a sequence number and label:

```
USE TRIAL
OUTPUT TEMP
FOR I=1 TO 5
   PRINT X(I),I,SEX$
NEXT
RUN
```

Then, read the data from the text file TEMP into a SYSTAT file NEWTRIAL:

```
OUTPUT *
NEW
GET TEMP
INPUT X,I,SEX$
SAVE NEWTRIAL
RUN
```

A listing of NEWTRIAL produces:

```
                       X           I          SEX$

CASE      1         10.000       1.000          Male
CASE      2         20.000       2.000          Male
CASE      3         30.000       3.000          Male
CASE      4         40.000       4.000          Male
CASE      5         50.000       5.000          Male
CASE      6         11.000       1.000        Female
CASE      7         21.000       2.000        Female
CASE      8         31.000       3.000        Female
CASE      9         41.000       4.000        Female
CASE     10         51.000       5.000        Female
```

See the next chapter, **Rearranging and combining files**, for more sophisticated data manipulation of this sort.

5 Rearranging and combining files

Rearranging and combining files 5

Overview

In this chapter, you will learn how to do various file manipulation tasks including merging files, dropping variables, selecting subsets of variables, deleting cases, and rearranging variables.

APPEND *file1 file2*	Creates a new file (named by a SAVE command) by appending cases of *file2* at the bottom after cases of *file1*. Both files must contain the same variables, in the same order, but they can have different numbers of cases. You must use SAVE before APPEND, which is HOT.
DELETE	Prevents the current case from being written to the SAVE file.
DROP *varlist*	Prevents the variables given by *varlist* from being written to the file named by SAVE.
TRANSPOSE	Transposes a data file by turning rows (cases) into columns (variables) and vice versa. You can only transpose files with numeric data. TRANSPOSE can handle a maximum of 99 cases (before transposing).
USE *file1* [(*varlist*)] *file2* [(*varlist*)]	Brings both *file1* and *file2* into the active workspace. You can merge these files into a single third file. Use the optional *varlists* if you want to merge only portions of the file(s).
USE *filename* (*varlist*)	Retrieves the specified variables from the SYSTAT file *filename*.

Dropping variables

To produce a file that contains a subset of variables from an existing file, you can either drop variables with the DROP command or select a subset of variables with the USE command.

DROP takes a *varlist* argument: follow the word DROP with the name(s) of the variable(s) you want to omit. Examples are:

```
DROP DEAD
DROP OUT
```

Imagine a file called OLDFILE that contains the variables WANTED and UNWANTED. Both of the following procedures create a file NEWFILE that contains only the variable WANTED:

```
USE OLDFILE              USE OLDFILE(WANTED)
DROP UNWANTED            SAVE NEWFILE
SAVE NEWFILE             RUN
RUN
```

The USE command extracts a small number of variables from a large file most easily. To delete a small number of variables from a large file, the DROP command is more convenient.

We illustrate both methods below.

5.1
Dropping two variables

Here, we drop the variables A and B from a file DATASET that contains:

		A	B	C	D
Case	1	1.000	2.000	3.000	4.000
Case	2	5.000	6.000	7.000	8.000
Case	3	9.000	1.000	2.000	3.000
Case	4	4.000	5.000	6.000	7.000
Case	5	8.000	9.000	1.000	2.000

The following program saves only C and D into NEWDATA:

```
USE DATASET
SAVE NEWDATA
DROP A B
RUN
```

To see the contents of NEWDATA, enter:

```
USE NEWDATA
LIST
RUN
```

```
                          C           D

 Case     1             3.000       4.000
 Case     2             7.000       8.000
 Case     3             2.000       3.000
 Case     4             6.000       7.000
 Case     5             1.000       2.000
```

Note: after you list a variable in a DROP command, you cannot refer to it in any other **DATA** command. For this reason you should usually make DROP the last **DATA** command you issue before RUN. For example, the following produces an error message about using an uninitialized variable.

```
DROP X
LET X2=X^2
RUN
```

5.2
Extracting three variables

You can select subsets of variables with the USE command. Here, we save the variables SPIRITS, WINE, and BEER from the dataset USDATA into a file called LIQUOR.

```
USE USDATA(SPIRITS WINE BEER)
SAVE LIQUOR
RUN
```

SYSTAT responds by listing only the variables you specified:

```
SYSTAT file variables available to you are:
   SPIRITS            WINE             BEER
```


When you type RUN, SYSTAT responds:

```
   50 cases and    3 variables processed.
SYSTAT file created.
```

Now enter:

```
USE LIQUOR
```

When you issue this USE command, SYSTAT shows that the variables you selected previously are the only ones in the file:

```
SYSTAT file variables available to you are:
   SPIRITS           WINE           BEER
```

Reordering variables

You can reorder variables in a SYSTAT file with the USE command by specifying the variables in their new order enclosed in parentheses.

5.3
Rearranging three variables

This example extracts the variables SPIRITS, WINE, and BEER from USDATA and rearranges them in the new file ALCOHOL.

```
USE USDATA(BEER SPIRITS WINE)
SAVE ALCOHOL
RUN
```

Now enter the following:

```
USE ALCOHOL
```

```
SYSTAT file variables available to you are:
      BEER        SPIRITS           WINE
```

The variables are now in the order we specified in the USE command, not in their previous USDATA order (SPIRITS, WINE, BEER).

Deleting cases

The DELETE command prevents cases from being saved into a file. It can be used selectively with an IF...THEN statement.

Examples:

```
IF CASE=10 THEN DELETE
IF GROUP>3 THEN DELETE
```

SYSTAT prevents the cases you identify from being saved into a new file. You cannot remove cases from the original file. Rather, you must create a new file that contains all the data in the original file except for the cases that you tell SYSTAT to delete.

5.4
Deleting cases

The following program causes SYSTAT to create a file NEWDATA that contains only the last 5 cases of USDATA. We list the variable STATE$ to show the cases SYSTAT has saved.

```
USE USDATA
SAVE NEWDATA
IF CASE<=45 THEN DELETE
LIST STATE$
RUN
```

```
                    STATE$

Case    46                    WA
Case    47                    OR
Case    48                    CA
Case    49                    AK
Case    50                    HI

    5 cases and    43 variables processed.
SYSTAT file created.
```

These are the cases SYSTAT has saved. In the new file, it renumbers them as cases 1–5:

```
                    STATE$

Case     1                    WA
Case     2                    OR
Case     3                    CA
Case     4                    AK
Case     5                    HI
```


5.5 Saving certain cases

The following program saves into NEWFILE only those cases in USDATA where DIVISION equals 2 or 4.

```
USE USDATA
SAVE NEWFILE
IF DIVISION<>2 AND DIVISION<>4 THEN DELETE
LIST DIVISION
RUN
```

```
                    DIVISION

 Case     7              2.000
 Case     8              2.000
 Case     9              2.000
 Case    15              4.000
 Case    16              4.000
 Case    17              4.000
 Case    18              4.000
 Case    19              4.000
 Case    20              4.000
 Case    21              4.000

   10 cases and   43 variables processed.
SYSTAT file created.
```

Transposing a file

The TRANSPOSE command transposes the cases and variables of a file. The command has no arguments. Just type it before you RUN. You must SAVE to a new file, however, to retain the transposed file.

You cannot transpose a file that contains a character variable unless the character variable is named LABEL$ and is the first variable in the file. In this instance TRANSPOSE uses the values in LABEL$ to label the variables in the transposed file.

You cannot transpose a file with more than 99 cases. Transposing a symmetric matrix (e.g. correlations) is unnecessary since the transpose of a symmetric matrix is the original matrix.

The transposed file contains an additional character variable called LABEL$ that contains the old variable names. The names for the columns in the new transposed file are COL(01–*n*) where *n* is the number of cases you had in the matrix to be transposed.

RANK, SORT, STANDARDIZE, and TRANSPOSE cannot be used jointly in one step (one RUN). If you want to STANDARDIZE and then TRANSPOSE, for example, do something like the following:

```
USE FILE1
SAVE FILE2
STANDARDIZE
RUN

USE FILE2
SAVE FILE3
TRANSPOSE
RUN
```

You can transpose a transposed file. This standardizes MYFILE by rows:

```
USE MYFILE
SAVE TFILE
TRANSPOSE
RUN

USE TFILE
SAVE SFILE
STANDARDIZE
RUN

USE SFILE
SAVE MYFILE
TRANSPOSE
RUN
```

MYFILE is standardized within rows but otherwise is the same.

Combining files

There are two ways to combine files: ***horizontally*** (side-by-side, concatenating different variables for the same cases) and ***vertically*** (end-to-end, concatenating different cases for the same variables).

The USE command performs horizontal concatenation:

```
USE A B
SAVE C
RUN
```

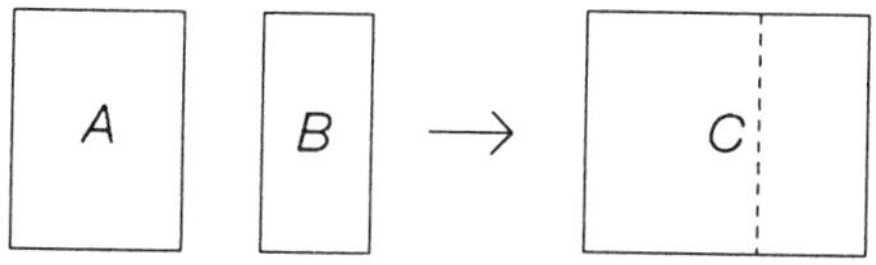

The APPEND command performs vertical concatenation.

```
SAVE C
APPEND A B
```

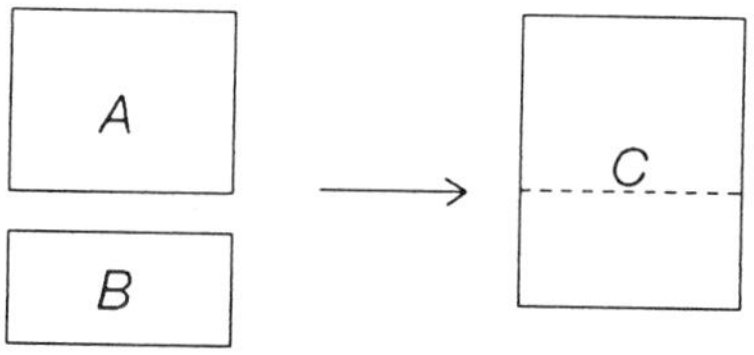

The APPEND command does not require RUN to execute. You can merge or append only two files at one time. If you have more than two files, merge them successively, two at a time, until they are all part of one file.

Merging horizontally

The USE command allows you to join two SYSTAT files horizontally (side-by-side). SYSTAT produces a file containing the variables in the first file followed by the unique variables in the second file. If you do not specify any index variable(s), SYSTAT matches the cases from the two files in order, matching the first case from each file, then the second case from each file, and so on until the last case. If one file has more observations than the other, SYSTAT assigns missing values to the variables from the shorter file for all the unmatched observations. If the same variable name appears in both files, SYSTAT uses the values from the second file, thus overwriting the values for the same variable in the first file.

The total number of variables in the two files cannot exceed the number allowed in a single SYSTAT file.

You can subset and reorder variables when you merge, e.g.:

```
USE MOE(X Y Z) JOE(C A B)
USE MOE(Z) JOE
USE MOE JOE(A B)
```

The first example merges two files, extracting variables X, Y, and Z from MOE and variables C, A, and B from JOE. The second selects variable Z from MOE and all the variables in JOE. The third selects all the variables from MOE and A and B from JOE.

Merging by key variables

You can merge files using a key (index) variable (or several key variables). You must sort both files on the key variable(s) before merging.

SYSTAT matches the cases that have the same values for the key variable(s) and merges them in a case in the new file. If there are values for the key variable(s) in one file and not the other, the merged file records missing values for the variable whose file did not have values. Here is an example:

```
USE A B/KEY
SAVE C
RUN
```

File A		*File B*		*File C*		
KEY	X	KEY	Y	KEY	X	Y
1	10	1	100	1	10	100
2	20	3	300	2	20	.
				3	.	300

One key variable may have many occurrences of a value that appears only once in the other file. For this, SYSTAT replicates the values from the other file. For example:

File KIDS		*File MOMS*		*File PAIRS*		
FAMILY	X	FAMILY	Y	FAMILY	X	Y
1	10	1	100	1	10	100
1	11			1	11	100
1	12			1	12	100

5.6 MERGE example

This example demonstrates merging two files with USE. One file, NAME, contains the names of men who have been presidential candidates in the variable NAME$. The second file, PARTY, contains their party affiliations in the variable PARTY$:

```
NAME$        PARTY$

Eisenhower   Republican
Stevenson    Democrat
Kennedy      Democrat
Goldwater    Republican
Johnson      Democrat
Humphrey     Democrat
McGovern     Democrat
Nixon        Republican
Ford         Republican
Carter       Democrat
Reagan       Republican
Bush         Republican
```

A one-to-one correspondence exists between the cases in the two files. The first case from the NAME file corresponds with the first case in the PARTY file. Now we can merge these files into a file called CANDIDAT.

```
USE NAME PARTY
SAVE CANDIDAT
LIST
RUN
```

When you issue the USE command, SYSTAT lists the variables from both files:

```
SYSTAT file variables available to you are:
     NAME$          PARTY$
```

When you type RUN, SYSTAT responds:

```
                         NAME$        PARTY$

Case      1        Eisenhower   Republican
Case      2         Stevenson     Democrat
Case      3           Kennedy     Democrat
Case      4         Goldwater   Republican
Case      5           Johnson     Democrat
Case      6          Humphrey     Democrat
Case      7          McGovern     Democrat
Case      8             Nixon   Republican
Case      9              Ford   Republican
Case     10            Carter     Democrat
Case     11            Reagan   Republican
Case     12              Bush   Republican

   12 cases and    2 variables processed.
SYSTAT file created.
```

5.7 Merging with a key variable

This example merges the files ELECTION and CANDIDAT by the variable NAME$. CANDIDAT was created in Example 5.6. Now we can make ELECTION.

```
SAVE ELECTION
INPUT NAME$, LOSER$, YEAR
RUN
Eisenhower Stevenson  1952
Eisenhower Stevenson  1956
Kennedy    Nixon      1960
Johnson    Goldwater  1964
Nixon      Humphrey   1968
Nixon      McGovern   1972
Carter     Ford       1976
Reagan     Carter     1980
Reagan     Mondale    1984
Bush       Dukakis    1988
~
```

YEAR designates the year of the presidential election, NAME$ the candidate who won that year, and LOSER$ the candidate who lost.

First, sort CANDIDAT and ELECTION:

```
USE CANDIDAT
SAVE CANDSORT
SORT NAME$
RUN
USE ELECTION
SAVE ELECSORT
SORT NAME$
RUN
```

To merge by NAME$, USE both sorted files in a single command and specify the key variable, NAME$.

```
USE ELECSORT CANDSORT/NAME$
SAVE MERGFILE
RUN
```

A LIST of MERGFILE reads:

		NAME$	LOSER$	YEAR	PARTY$
Case	1	Bush	Dukakis	1988.000	Republican
Case	2	Carter	Ford	1976.000	Democrat
Case	3	Eisenhower	Stevenson	1952.000	Republican
Case	4	Eisenhower	Stevenson	1956.000	Republican
Case	5	Ford		.	Republican
Case	6	Goldwater		.	Republican
Case	7	Humphrey		.	Democrat
Case	8	Johnson	Goldwater	1964.000	Democrat
Case	9	Kennedy	Nixon	1960.000	Democrat
Case	10	McGovern		.	Democrat
Case	11	Nixon	Humphrey	1968.000	Republican
Case	12	Nixon	McGovern	1972.000	Republican
Case	13	Reagan	Carter	1980.000	Republican
Case	14	Reagan	Mondale	1984.000	Republican
Case	15	Stevenson		.	Democrat

The missing values occur where entries in CANDIDAT have no matching value for NAME$ in ELECTION (e.g. Ford, Goldwater, Humphrey, etc. did not win). SYSTAT sets to missing the variables that came from ELECTION (LOSER$ and YEAR) for these cases. The ELECTION file has three names that have more than one entry: Eisenhower, Nixon, and Reagan. In these cases, SYSTAT replicates the corresponding values from CANDIDAT.

Note: if you subset variables while merging, you must include the key variable(s) in both subsets. For example, the first command below works, and the second command does not.

```
USE INDOOR(TIME,LOC,CO2) OUTDOOR(TIME,LOC,NOX)/TIME,LOC
USE INDOOR(TIME,LOC,CO2) OUTDOOR(NOX)/TIME,LOC
```

Appending vertically

APPEND joins two files vertically. The files must have the same variables in the same order. SYSTAT places cases from the second file you name below those from the first.

Examples are:

```
SAVE FINANCE
APPEND SALES UPDATES

SAVE PEOPLE
APPEND MALES FEMALES
```

APPEND is HOT, like RUN. SYSTAT executes APPEND immediately. To save the appended files permanently, issue a SAVE command before APPEND. SAVE is the only prior command that affects APPEND.

5.8 APPEND example

Here are two SYSTAT files, named MEN and WOMEN:

MEN

SEX$	AGE
MALE	18.000
MALE	35.000
MALE	24.000
MALE	20.000

WOMEN

SEX$	AGE
FEMALE	23.000
FEMALE	40.000
FEMALE	40.000
FEMALE	31.000

To append them into a file named SEXES, type:

```
SAVE SEXES
APPEND WOMEN MEN
```

```
    8 cases and    2 variables processed.
SYSTAT file created.
```

The new file contains:

		SEX$	AGE
Case	1	FEMALE	23.000
Case	2	FEMALE	40.000
Case	3	FEMALE	26.000
Case	4	FEMALE	31.000
Case	5	MALE	18.000
Case	6	MALE	35.000
Case	7	MALE	24.000
Case	8	MALE	20.000

SYSTAT placed the cases from WOMEN before those from MEN because we listed WOMEN first in the APPEND command.

6 Transforming variables

Transforming variables 6

Overview

This chapter shows you how to perform simple transformations of your data. You can do many of the transformations using the Data Editor (see the *Getting Started* manual). For repetitive transformations or more complex programs, though, you need **DATA**, with the LET and IF...THEN commands.

With **DATA**, you can also recode variables using CODE and create character equivalents of numeric variables using LABEL. All of these transformations can be used in more complex programs, which are discussed in the next chapter.

CODE *varlist* / *old1=new1, old2=new2, ..., oldp=newp*	Recodes the variables listed in *varlist*. For all the variables in *varlist*, any case with value *old1* is replaced with value *new1*. All occurrences of *old2* are replaced with *new2*, etc. All variables in *varlist* must be the same type (character or numeric), and the *oldp* and *newp* values must correspond to the variable type. Surround character strings with single or double quotation marks.
IF *exprn* **THEN** *statement*	Executes *statement* if the *exprn* evaluates as true. *Exprn* may be any valid expression formed with numbers, variables, operators, and functions. *Statement* may be any valid command, including DELETE.
LABEL *varlist* / *old1=label1, old2=label2, ..., oldp=labelp*	Creates a character variable for each numeric variable in *varlist*. *Varlist* can contain numeric variables only. For each numeric variable, a character variable with the same name plus $ is created, with values as given by *oldi=labeli*. If any character variable already exists, its values are replaced.
LET *var=exprn*	Assigns the value of *exprn* to the variable *var*. You may use either a numeric or character variable. Character values must be surrounded by single or double quotation marks.

The statements in this chapter allow you to do things like:

1) Re-express variables, e.g.

```
LET WEIGHT = LOG(WEIGHT)
```

2) Create new variables, e.g.

```
LET GRADE = QUIZ1+QUIZ2 + 2*FINAL
```

3) Create grouping variables, e.g.

```
IF AGE>21 THEN LET AGE$ = 'ADULT'
```

4) Create value labels for numeric codes, e.g.

```
LABEL SEX / 1='Female',2='Male'
```

5) Recode variable categories, e.g.

```
CODE GAUL / 1=1,2=1,3=2
```

How to transform

You generally do transformations this way:

```
USE filename
transformations
SAVE newfile
RUN
```

DATA does not execute transformations until you type RUN. This allows you to do many transformations at once. The file that you SAVE contains all the data in the original file plus any changes or additions that you make. In **DATA**, this saved file automatically becomes the file in use. If you want to go back to the original file, you must USE it again.

To retain transformed data permanently, you ***must*** save your work to a new file. If you do not explicitly specify a SAVE file, **DATA** stores the results of a run in a temporary data file which then becomes the active file. It stays open as you move from module to module. SYSTAT erases this temporary file when you execute a USE, SAVE, or QUIT command.

You cannot save to the file in use. The Data Editor allows you to save to the same file that you opened, but **DATA** does ***not***. To save the results of transformations, you ***must*** name a ***new*** file with a SAVE command sometime before you type RUN.

If you insist on saving to the original file, you can do so by executing the transformations, issuing a SAVE, and typing RUN again:

```
USE DEJAVU
transformations
RUN
SAVE DEJAVU
RUN
```

DATA makes use of operators and functions in expressions. An operator or function tells **DATA** to execute an operation or comparison on specified values or variables.

The operators and functions available are the same ones that are available in the Data Editor. They are listed with brief explanations here. Note that logs to the base 10 are the same as LOG(X)/LOG(10). Similarly, logs to the base 2 are the same as LOG(X)/LOG(2). The trigonometric functions (SIN, COS, etc.) are in radians. To use degrees, re-express like this: SIN(X*6.283/360)

Arithmetic operators

+	addition
–	subtraction
*	multiplication
/	division
^	exponentiation
–	unary minus (negative)

Functions

SQR	square root
LOG	natural logarithm
EXP	exponential function
ABS	absolute value
SIN	sine
COS	cosine
TAN	tangent
ASN	arcsine
ACS	arccosine
ATN	arctangent
ATH	arc hyperbolic tangent (Fisher's *z*)
INT	integer truncation
LAG	lag (shift values down one case)
LGM	log gamma

Relational operators

<	less than
=	equal to
>	greater than
<>	not equal to
<=	less than or equal to
=>	greater than or equal to

Logical operators

AND	logical and
OR	logical or
NOT	logical not

Multi-variable functions

AVG	mean of nonmissing values
SUM	sum of nonmissing values
MIN	minimum value of values
MAX	maximum value of values
STD	standard deviation of nonmissing values
MIS	number of missing values

Distribution functions

Distribution	*Cumulative*	*Density*	*Inverse*	*Random data*
Uniform	UCF(*x*)	UDF(*x*)	UIF(α)	URN
Normal	ZCF(*z*)	ZDF(*z*)	ZIF(α)	ZRN
t	TCF(*t*,*df*)	TDF(*t*,*df*)	TIF(α,*df*)	TRN(*df*)
F	FCF(*F*,*df1*,*df2*)	FDF(*F*,*df1*,*df2*)	FIF(α,*df1*,*df2*)	FRN(*df1*,*df2*)
Chi-square	XCF(χ^2,*df*)	XDF(χ^2,*df*)	XIF(α,*df*)	XRN(*df*)
Gamma	GCF(γ*p*)	GDF(γ*p*)	GIF(α,*p*)	GRN(*p*)
Beta	BCF(β,*p*,*q*)	BDF(β,*p*,*q*)	BIF(α,*p*,*q*)	BRN(*p*,*q*)
Exponential	ECF(*x*)	EDF(*x*)	EIF(α)	ERN
Logistic	LCF(*x*)	LDF(*x*)	LIF(α)	LRN
Studentized	SCF(*x*,*k*,*df*)	SDF(*x*,*k*,*df*)	SIF(α,*k*,*df*)	SRN(*k*,*df*)
Weibull	WCF(*x*,*p*,*q*)	WDF(*x*,*p*,*q*)	WIF(α,*p*,*q*)	WRN(*p*,*q*)
Binonmial	NCF(*x*,*n*,*p*)	NDF(*x*,*n*,*p*)	NIF(α,*n*,*p*)	NRN(*n*,*p*)
Poisson	PCF(*x*,*p*)	PDF(*x*,*p*)	PIF(α,*p*)	PRN(*p*)

The ZRN function, for example, generates random values from a normal distribution (*z* scores). If you used one of these scores in the ZCF function, the result would be the area under the normal curve to the left of this score. If you entered this area in the ZIF function, the original *z* score would be returned.

Built-in variables

Built-in variables allow you to index aspects of files:

BOF	beginning of file
EOF	end of file
BOG	beginning of group
EOG	end of group
CASE	case (observation) number

BOG and EOG are defined only with an associated BY statement. See the **Subgroup processing** chapter for more information.

Order of operations

Expressions are evaluated from left to right according to the precedence of operators. That is, operators with higher precedence are evaluated before those with lower precedence, and if there are "ties," operators appearing first in the equations are evaluated first. Order of precedence from highest to lowest runs as follows:

1) Expressions enclosed in parentheses	( )
2) Exponentiation	^
3) Unary minus, logical negation	–, NOT
4) Multiplication and division	*, /
5) Addition and subtraction	+, –
6) Relational operators	=, <>, <, >, <=, >=
7) Logical operators	AND, OR

Missing values

Missing character data values appear in SYSTAT commands and output as blanks. Missing numeric data values appear as periods (.). SYSTAT stores missing numeric data as negative values less than any number allowed in SYSTAT arithmetic, –1.0E36. This is because all logical comparisons, including < and >, must evaluate to TRUE (1) or FALSE (0). Otherwise, statements such as GOTO would not work properly.

Note: Logic operations with missing values have changed since prior versions.

Comparisons with missing numeric data evaluate as follows:

. AND T	is missing	. OR T	is true
. AND F	is false	. OR F	is missing
. AND .	is missing	. OR .	is missing
NOT .	is missing		
. < .	is missing	. = T	is false
. < T	is missing	. <> .	is false
. = .	is true	. <> T	is true

Notice that logical values can evaluate to missing. In IF statements, missing and false both result in the THEN statement being shipped and the ELSE statement (if any) executed.

All numeric arithmetic expressions involving missing values propagate missing values. For example, if you have two variables X and Y in a SYSTAT file and you sum them as follows:

```
LET TOTAL = X + Y
```

the value for the new variable TOTAL is missing for every case where either X or Y or both are missing.

Y	X	TOTAL
1	1	2
2	.	.
.	3	.
.	.	.

Only the multi-variable functions AVG, SUM, MIN, MAX, and STD automatically exclude missing values from computations.

Simple transformations using LET

The LET statement has the format:

```
LET var=exprn
```

SYSTAT assigns the value of the expression *exprn* to the variable named by *var*. Examples of LET statements are:

```
LET X=2
LET X=Y
LET X=Y+2
LET RATE=CARDIO+CANCER
LET LCARDIO=LOG(CARDIO)
```

You can use LET to transform an existing variable or to create new variables. The expression on the right side of the equal sign can be any general mathematical expression on real numbers or characters. If an expression results in an illegal value (as would dividing by zero), SYSTAT sets the value for that case to missing. Also, missing values in arithmetic propagate missing values (e.g., 2 + . = .).

Any variable that you use on the right of the equal sign must exist in the file. If it does not, SYSTAT displays the following error message:

```
Warning: you are using an uninitialized variable.
Its value will be set to missing.
```

You can execute only one transformation with one LET command. For instance, SYSTAT does not allow statements like the following:

```
LET X=2 AND Y=3
LET X=2 AND LET Y=3
```

SYSTAT *does* allow the following expression, however:

```
LET OK = X=2 AND Y=3
```

This statement shows two uses of the equal sign. The first is the equal sign designating *assignment* of the computed value to the variable OK. The second two are relational operators. The value of OK will be 1 for any case where X is 2 and Y is 3. Otherwise, its value will be 0.

6.1 Re-expression

In the following program the values of the variable CARDIO in the file USDATA are transformed into their natural logs. The first ten values of CARDIO are:

```
                    CARDIO

Case    1         466.200
Case    2         395.900
Case    3         433.100
Case    4         460.600
Case    5         474.100
Case    6         423.800
Case    7         499.500
Case    8         464.700
Case    9         508.700
Case   10         443.100
```

To calculate the natural logs of these values, first USE the file, enter the LET statement, specify a SAVE file, and then set it all in motion with RUN:

```
USE USDATA
LET CARDIO = LOG(CARDIO)
SAVE NEWDATA
RUN
```

To list the first 10 transformed values of CARDIO, type:

```
REPEAT 10
LIST CARDIO
RUN
```

```
                    CARDIO

Case     1           6.145
Case     2           5.981
Case     3           6.071
Case     4           6.133
Case     5           6.161
Case     6           6.049
Case     7           6.214
Case     8           6.141
Case     9           6.232
Case    10           6.094

   10 cases and    43 variables processed.
No SYSTAT file created.
```

6.2 Creating new variables

In the above example, we transformed the values of CARDIO to equal their natural logs. The original values were not saved. To save both the original and natural log values of CARDIO, issue a LET statement to create a new variable instead of transforming an existing one.

```
NEW
USE USDATA
LET LCARDIO = LOG(CARDIO)
SAVE NEWFILE
RUN
```

To list the first 10 cases of both CARDIO and LCARDIO, type:

```
REPEAT 10
LIST CARDIO, LCARDIO
RUN
```

```
                    CARDIO       LCARDIO

Case     1          466.200        6.145
Case     2          395.900        5.981
Case     3          433.100        6.071
Case     4          460.600        6.133
Case     5          474.100        6.161
Case     6          423.800        6.049
Case     7          499.500        6.214
Case     8          464.700        6.141
Case     9          508.700        6.232
Case    10          443.100        6.094

   10 cases and    44 variables processed.
No SYSTAT file created.
```

6.3
Multiple LET statements

You can execute many transformation statements at once. The following program executes three transformations and saves the results into a file called NEWDATA:

```
USE USDATA
LET LCARDIO = LOG(CARDIO)
LET RATE = CARDIO+CANCER
LET ALCOHOL = SPIRITS+WINE+BEER
SAVE NEWDATA
RUN
```

Note that each transformation is on its own line. You may include only one transformation, such as a LET statement, per line.

IF...THEN LET

With the IF...THEN statement, you can execute conditional transformations. The format for an IF...THEN statement is:

```
IF condition THEN LET expression
```

Examples are:

```
IF X=99 THEN LET X=.
IF CARDIO>400 AND 100<CANCER THEN LET RATE$='EXTREME'
```

6.4
Simple conditional transformation

The average value for the variable CARDIO is approximately 398 with a standard deviation of 84. To indicate states where CARDIO is more than one standard deviation greater than the mean, use a conditional transformation statement as follows:

```
USE USDATA
SAVE NEWFILE
IF CARDIO>482 THEN LET RATE$='HIGH'
RUN
```

```
   50 cases and   44 variables processed.
SYSTAT file created.
```

Now list the first ten cases for the variables CARDIO and RATE$ in NEWFILE by typing:

```
REPEAT 10
LIST CARDIO, RATE$
RUN
```

```
                        CARDIO        RATE$

 Case      1              466.200
 Case      2              395.900
 Case      3              433.100
 Case      4              460.600
 Case      5              474.100
 Case      6              423.800
 Case      7              499.500          HIGH
 Case      8              464.700
 Case      9              508.700          HIGH
 Case     10              443.100

    10 cases and    44 variables processed.
 No SYSTAT file created.
```

Two of the first ten cases in the file meet the condition CARDIO>482; for these cases SYSTAT assigns the value "HIGH" to the new variable RATE$. For all cases that do not meet the condition, SYSTAT sets RATE$ to blank, indicating a missing value.

6.5 IF...THEN using logical OR

The average value for the variable CANCER in the data set USDATA is approximately 178, with a standard deviation of 33. To create a variable that indicates states whose values are more than one standard deviation above the average for CARDIO *or* CANCER *or* both, use the following transformation program:

```
USE USDATA
SAVE NEWFILE
IF CARDIO>482 OR CANCER>211 THEN LET RATE$='HIGH'
LIST CARDIO CANCER RATE$
RUN
```

Here is a listing of the first 10 cases:

```
                    CARDIO      CANCER        RATE$

Case     1         466.200     213.800         HIGH
Case     2         395.900     182.200
Case     3         433.100     188.100
Case     4         460.600     219.000         HIGH
Case     5         474.100     231.500         HIGH
Case     6         423.800     205.100
Case     7         499.500     209.900         HIGH
Case     8         464.700     216.300         HIGH
Case     9         508.700     223.600         HIGH
Case    10         443.100     198.800
```

Now, for every case where CARDIO is greater than 482 *or* CANCER is greater than 211 *or* both, SYSTAT assigns RATE$ a value of HIGH.

6.6
IF...THEN using logical AND

To create a variable that indicates those cases where both CARDIO *and* CANCER are more than one standard deviation above the average, type the following:

```
USE USDATA
SAVE NEWFILE
IF CARDIO>492 AND CANCER>211 THEN LET RATE$='HIGH'
LIST CARDIO, CANCER, RATE$
RUN
```

Here are the first 10 transformed cases:

```
                    CARDIO      CANCER        RATE$

Case     1         466.200     213.800
Case     2         395.900     182.200
Case     3         433.100     188.100
Case     4         460.600     219.000
Case     5         474.100     231.500
Case     6         423.800     205.100
Case     7         499.500     209.900
Case     8         464.700     216.300
Case     9         508.700     223.600         HIGH
Case    10         443.100     198.800
```

Only one of the first ten cases has both CARDIO greater than 482 *and* CANCER greater than 211.

Recoding values using CODE

The CODE command provides a convenient way to recode or collapse categories of categorical values.

Examples are:

```
CODE REGION, DIVISION/1=2, 3=2, 4=1
CODE STATE$/'NY'='East of Eden', 'IL'='Eden','CA'='West
   of Eden'
```

You can reference more than one variable in a CODE command, but you cannot mix numeric and character variables in the same CODE statement. To create a character variable from a numeric variable, use LABEL or a series of IF...THEN statements.

You can also execute conditional codes as follows:

```
IF exprn THEN FOR
   CODE specification
NEXT
```

See the next chapter for more information about this type of statement.

The syntax of the CODE statement is:

```
CODE varlist / oldvalue1=newvalue1,
  oldvalue2=newvalue2,...
```

You must be careful about the order in which you specify the recoding because SYSTAT recodes in the order that you list the changes. For instance, if you incorrectly enter:

```
CODE REGION/1=2, 2=3, 3=1
```

SYSTAT recodes REGION to 1 for all cases where REGION is 1, 2, or 3. It first codes all 1's to 2's, then all 2's to 3's (including those that had just been changed from 1 to 2), and then all 3's back to 1's. Here's a correct way to change 1's to 2's, 2's to 3's, and 3's to 1's.

```
CODE REGION/1=11, 2=12, 3=1, 11=2, 12=3
```

In this way, all 1's are changed to 11's, then all 2's to 12's, then all 3's to 1's, then 11's to 2's, and finally 12's to 3's.

Note to SPSS users: the syntax of this statement resembles, but is not identical to, the SPSS RECODE statement. The value on the left of each equal sign is recoded into the value on the right. If you want to recode several values into the same value, use several equal signs as in the example above. To recode continuous variables into categories, use a series of IF...THEN statements as shown at the end of the **Tables** chapter.

6.7
Simple CODE

In the dataset USDATA, the first 14 cases contain states in divisions 1, 2, and 3. The following program copies the division values into the variable DIVISN2 and changes these values so that 1=3, 2=1, and 3=2.

```
USE USDATA
SAVE NEWFILE
REPEAT 14
  LET DIVISN2=DIVISION
  CODE DIVISN2/1=11, 2=12,3=2, 11=3, 12=1
RUN
```

The values for the first 14 cases of DIVISION and DIVISN2 in the data set NEWFILE are:

		DIVISION	DIVISN2
Case	1	1.000	3.000
Case	2	1.000	3.000
Case	3	1.000	3.000
Case	4	1.000	3.000
Case	5	1.000	3.000
Case	6	1.000	3.000
Case	7	2.000	1.000
Case	8	2.000	1.000
Case	9	2.000	1.000
Case	10	3.000	2.000
Case	11	3.000	2.000
Case	12	3.000	2.000
Case	13	3.000	2.000
Case	14	3.000	2.000

6.8
Conditional
CODE

In USDATA, the first 9 cases contain states in region 1. The following program executes the recode from the previous example only for those states where REGION equals 1. The FOR ... NEXT statement is explained in the next chapter. This example should illustrate its use for recodes, however.

```
USE USDATA
SAVE NEWFILE
LET DIVISN2=DIVISION
IF REGION=1 THEN FOR
   CODE DIVISN2/1=11, 2=12, 3=2, 11=3, 12=1
NEXT
RUN
```

Comparing the original and recoded values of DIVISION shows that SYSTAT has recoded only those values where REGION=1:

			original	*recoded*
		REGION	DIVISION	DIVISN2
Case	1	1.000	1.000	3.000
Case	2	1.000	1.000	3.000
Case	3	1.000	1.000	3.000
Case	4	1.000	1.000	3.000
Case	5	1.000	1.000	3.000
Case	6	1.000	1.000	3.000
Case	7	1.000	2.000	1.000
Case	8	1.000	2.000	1.000
Case	9	1.000	2.000	1.000
Case	10	2.000	3.000	3.000
Case	11	2.000	3.000	3.000
Case	12	2.000	3.000	3.000
Case	13	2.000	3.000	3.000
Case	14	2.000	3.000	3.000

Creating character variables using LABEL

The LABEL command creates a character variable whose values correspond to those of a numeric variable.

An example:

```
LABEL DIVISION/1='New England',2='Mid Atlantic',
  3='North Central'
```

LABEL names the new character variable by adding a dollar sign to the numeric variable's name. In the example above, LABEL DIVISION adds the variable DIVISION$ to your file. If DIVISION$ already exists in the file, SYSTAT replaces its values with those created by the LABEL command.

LABEL cannot create unique character variable names for subscripted variables. If you LABEL a subscripted variable, SYSTAT creates a counterpart character variable without the subscript. For example, if you use LABEL on the variable QUESTION(3), SYSTAT creates the character variable QUESTION$. Using LABEL with QUESTION(4) also produces QUESTION$.

You can use these new character variables in place of the numeric variables in any SYSTAT statistical procedure that allows value labels, such as **TABLES**. For example, you can use the following statement to make value labels in **DATA**:

```
LABEL SEX/1='Male',2='Female'
```

and then you can tabulate SEX$ with the TABULATE command in **TABLES**.

6.9
Simple LABEL

Create the file GENDER with the following commands:

```
SAVE GENDER
INPUT SEX
LABEL SEX/1='FEMALE', 2='MALE'
RUN
1
2
2
1
2
2
1
~
```


GENDER will contain two variables: SEX, which you entered by hand, and SEX$, which SYSTAT created from SEX:

```
                          SEX          SEX$

Case    1               1.000        FEMALE
Case    2               2.000          MALE
Case    3               2.000          MALE
Case    4               1.000        FEMALE
Case    5               2.000          MALE
Case    6               2.000          MALE
Case    7               1.000        FEMALE
```

Lagging with LAG

The LAG function shifts values down one row, replacing the first value with a missing value.

Examples are:

```
LET Y=LAG(X)
LET Z=LAG(LOG(X))
```

The first example produces a new variable Y whose values are those of X, shifted down one position:

X	Y
1	.
2	1
3	2
4	3

The second example produces a new variable Z whose values are the logs of X, shifted down one position.

You cannot LAG a variable twice in one run. For example, neither of the following would work.

```
LET Y=LAG(LAG(Y))
```

```
LET Y=LAG(X)
LET Z=LAG(Y)
```

If you want to lag a variable or expression twice, use successive runs:

```
LET Y=LAG(X)
RUN
LET Z=LAG(Y)
RUN
```

6.16
First order lag

Here we input a variable Y and lag its square.

```
INPUT Y
SAVE TEST
RUN
1
2
3
4
5
6
~

    6 cases and    1 variables processed
SYSTAT file created

USE TEST
LET Z=LAG(Y^2)
SAVE TEST2
RUN

    6 cases and    2 variables processed
SYSTAT file created

USE TEST2
LIST
RUN

                          Y           Z

  Case     1            1.000         .
  Case     2            2.000       1.000
  Case     3            3.000       4.000
  Case     4            4.000       9.000
  Case     5            5.000      16.000
  Case     6            6.000      25.000
```

7 Programming in SYSTAT

Programming in SYSTAT 7

Overview

This chapter provides general rules and guidelines for using the **DATA** BASIC data transformation language. You already learned the rudiments of BASIC in the previous chapter: LET for simple transformations, and IF...THEN for conditional transformations.

You do not need to use **DATA** BASIC for any but the most complicated transformations. The previous chapter discusses simple transformations, and the *Getting Started* volume gives instruction on doing transformations through the SYSTAT Data Editor.

Examples of BASIC programs are given in this chapter and in the **Programming examples** chapter.

DIM *var(n)*	Reserves space for a new variable *var* with subscript *n*, where *n* is an integer between 1 and 99 inclusive.
ELSE *statement*	Can follow an IF...THEN command. *Statement* is executed when the IF *exprn* evaluates as false. The *statement* can be any valid command, including DELETE or another IF...THEN command.
ERASE *n1*[–*n2*]	Erases all numbered BASIC statements from *n1* to *n2*, inclusive. The default, if no range is specified, is all numbered statements.
FOR [*index=n1* **TO** *n2* [STEP=*n3*]] ... **NEXT**	Starts a FOR...NEXT loop. *Index* must be a numeric variable, either from your file or a new variable. You must specify *n1*, but *n2* is optional. You may optionally specify an increment value with the STEP=*n3* phrase; the default is +1. You may specify any real number or expression for *n1–3*. See text for instructions on using FOR...NEXT with or without an *index*.
GOTO *n*	Detours the program to the statement numbered *n*. You must have numbered line statements in your program to use GOTO.
IF *exprn* **THEN** *statement*	Executes *statement* if the *exprn* evaluates as true. *Exprn* may be any valid expression formed with numbers, variables, operators, and functions. *Statement* may be any valid command, including DELETE.

LET *var=exprn*	Assigns the value of *exprn* to the variable *var*. You may use either a numeric or character variable. Character values must be surrounded by single or double quotation marks.
PRINT *varlist* | *'string'*	Displays the values of the variables listed in *varlist*, or displays the character *string* you specify. *Varlist* may include numeric or character variables. See Chapter 1 for information about using the *varlist* argument. Character string arguments are discussed in this chapter.
STOP	Stops execution of a BASIC program.

In the Data Editor, you must do transformations individually, and you are limited to simple "Set *variable* to *exprn*" transformations and simple conditional "If *exprn* then set *variable* to *exprn*" transformations. The previous chapter showed how you can do these simple transformations with **DATA**.

DATA BASIC lets you do more complicated tasks like the following:

Execute several transformations at one time
Use array (subscripted) variables
Do FOR...NEXT loops
Do IF...THEN...ELSE statements
Calculate unusual statistics such as trimmed means
Generate unusual random data sets.

General usage

You will typically use the following format for any **DATA** BASIC program:

```
USE filename
   BASIC program
   .
   .
   .
SAVE newfile
RUN
```

When you enter the RUN command, SYSTAT executes the BASIC program you have entered. SYSTAT runs the program once for each case in your data file.

Saving your work

Whenever you transform variables using **DATA** BASIC, you must SAVE the transformed values to a new file to preserve your work permanently. SYSTAT will not add the transformed values to the original file. If you do not SAVE to a new file, SYSTAT stores the results of your work in a temporary data file.

For example, the following program writes all the data in USDATA plus the variable X into NEWDATA, and NEWDATA becomes the active file. USDATA remains unchanged.

```
USE USDATA
LET X=LOG(CARDIO)
SAVE NEWDATA
RUN
```

When you issue the SAVE command, you must specify a file name different from the USE file. **DATA** does not let you write to the current file.

If you do not use a SAVE command before you type RUN, SYSTAT stores results in a temporary data file. This file becomes the active file, and all your commands refer to it until your next RUN command. If you enter more commands and another RUN without giving a SAVE statement, **DATA** overwrites the temporary data file.

The temporary data files remain in memory if you transfer back to the main SYSTAT procedures to do analyses. SYSTAT continues to use a temporary file until you USE a new file, SAVE to a file in **DATA**, open the Data Editor, or QUIT, at which point SYSTAT erases all temporary data files. All of this takes place invisibly.

The temporary data files allow you to do many RUNs without having to SAVE intermediate files. You can do all your data and file manipulations and then SAVE only the final version. For example:

```
USE A(X(1-5)) B
LET Z=LOG(Z)
STANDARDIZE X(1-5)
RUN
TRANSPOSE
RUN
etc.
SAVE FINAL
RUN
```

Line numbers

You may number the lines in your BASIC programs. Any time you begin a command with a line number in **DATA**, SYSTAT assumes you are entering a BASIC statement. A line number can be any integer between 0 and 32,000. You may increment line numbers by any amount. You can enter lines out of order, but SYSTAT executes them in increasing numerical order.

You do not need to give line numbers to BASIC statements. You may even mix numbered and unnumbered BASIC statements in one RUN. If you do, SYSTAT executes the unnumbered statements first, in the order you enter them. It then executes numbered statements in the order of their statement numbers.

Errors

When you enter a **DATA** BASIC statement, SYSTAT reads it and checks for syntax errors, and then stores it in memory for later execution. If SYSTAT finds an error, it tells you and lets you enter a new statement and continue programming. The statement with an error is forgotten.

Editing a BASIC program

Once you enter a BASIC program statement, you can change or erase it if you have given the statement a line number. Just enter a new statement with the same line number. SYSTAT forgets the first statement and uses the one you entered instead.

The following statements:

```
10 LET X=Y
20 LET A=X/10
10 LET X=Z
```

are stored as:

```
10 LET X=Z
20 LET A=X/10
```

Erasing BASIC statements

With the ERASE command you can remove numbered BASIC statements. If, in the above example, you type:

```
ERASE 10
```

SYSTAT eliminates statement 10 from the **DATA** BASIC program. This is equivalent to issuing a line number only:

```
10
```

The advantage of the ERASE command is that you can specify an entire range of BASIC statements. The following command removes all statements with numbers from 10 to 50:

```
ERASE 10-50
```

Statements and expressions

DATA BASIC makes use of operators and functions in expressions and statements. This section defines statements and expressions.

Operators and functions

DATA BASIC uses operators and functions in expressions. The operators and functions available are the same ones that are available in the Data Editor. See the **Transforming variables** chapter or the *Getting Started* manual for more information on these operators and functions.

Statements

A statement is a **DATA** BASIC command followed by its arguments:

```
command arguments
```

Examples are:

```
LET X=Y
GOTO 10
```

IF...THEN has a special format; the IF and THEN clauses each have arguments:

```
IF exprn THEN statement
```

Note that the argument for THEN is a statement. For example, legal IF...THEN statements are:

```
IF exprn THEN LET var = exprn
IF exprn THEN GOTO n
IF exprn THEN PRINT var|string
IF exprn THEN DELETE
IF exprn THEN IF exprn THEN...
IF exprn THEN FOR...
```

Note that IF...THEN can take another IF...THEN statement as its THEN statement.

Expressions

An expression is a combination of one or more variables (including special built-in variables), numbers, character strings, and/or operators which evaluates to some numeric or character value. There are three types of expressions: numeric, character, and relational.

Numeric expressions

Numeric expressions contain only numbers, variables, built-in variables (e.g., CASE), functions, operators, or combinations of these and evaluate to any real number which has a legal value in SYSTAT.

Examples of numeric expressions are:

```
2
2+2
SQR(2)
CARDIO
CARDIO+CANCER
SQR(CANCER)
```

Character expressions

Character expressions contain only character strings or character variables. When you use a character string or value as part of an expression, you must enclose that value in quotes. A character string cannot be longer than 12 characters.

Examples are:

```
'MALE'
"It's"
```

Relational expressions

The third type of expression is relational, or comparative. It compares either two numeric or two character expressions. It consists of two expressions of the same type joined by a relational operator (<, >, =, <=, >=, or <>). You cannot compare a numeric expression to a character expression.

Examples of relational expressions are:

```
REGION = 1
STATE$ <> 'NY'
CARDIO > CANCER
400 < (CARDIO+CANCER)
```

You may join a number of relational expressions together with the logical operators AND or OR to form complex relational expressions, e.g.:

```
CARDIO>100 OR CANCER>300
AGE<17 AND SEX$='FEMALE'
(AGE<17 OR AGE>60) AND SEX$='MALE'
```

You can also negate relational expressions with the logical operator NOT. NOT changes the value of a nonzero (true) expression to 0 (false) and the value of a 0 expression to 1. For example:

```
NOT (AGE>30 OR EXPERNCE>10 OR SCORE>80)
```

SYSTAT evaluates a relational expression for each case in your file. If the expression is true, SYSTAT assigns it a value of 1 for that case. If the expression is not true (is false), SYSTAT assigns it a value of 0 for that case. (SYSTAT follows the standard for programming languages and returns a 0 value for false and 1 for true. Microsoft BASIC is nonstandard and returns a value of 0 for false and minus 1 for true.)

For example, the following command gives X a value of 1 for every case where REGION is greater than 3 and a value of 0 for cases where REGION is 3 or less.

```
LET X=REGION>3
```

You can place a relational expression in the IF clause of an IF...THEN statement. If the expression evaluates to 1 (the expression is true), SYSTAT executes the statement following THEN. If the expression evaluates to 0 (the expression is not true), SYSTAT does not execute the statement.

Some valid IF...THEN statements:

```
IF SEX$='FEMALE' THEN LET GROUP=1
IF CARDIO>100 OR CANCER>300 THEN LET RATE$='HIGH'
IF GROUP=1 THEN GOTO 10
IF EDUCATN<12 THEN DELETE
IF REGION>3 AND CARDIO<300 THEN FOR
IF REGION>3 AND IF CARDIO<300 THEN FOR
```

Missing values

Missing character data values appear in SYSTAT commands and output as blanks. Missing numeric data values appear as periods (.). SYSTAT stores missing numeric data as negative values less than any number allowed in SYSTAT arithmetic, –1.0E36. This is because all logical comparisons, including < and >, must evaluate to TRUE (1) or FALSE (0). Otherwise, statements such as GOTO would not work properly.

Logical comparisons with missing numeric data evaluate as follows:

. AND T	is missing	**. OR T**	is true
. AND F	is false	**. OR F**	is missing
. AND .	is missing	**. OR .**	is missing
NOT .	is missing		
. < .	is missing	**. = T**	is missing
. < T	is missing	**. <> .**	is false
. = .	is true	**. <>T**	is true

All numeric arithmetic expressions involving missing values propagate missing values. For example, if you have two variables X and Y in a SYSTAT file and you sum them as follows:

```
LET TOTAL = X + Y
```

the value for the new variable TOTAL is missing for every case where either X or Y or both are missing.

Y	X	TOTAL
1	1	2
2	.	.
.	3	.
.	.	.

Only the multivariable functions AVG, SUM, MIN, MAX, and STD automatically exclude missing values from computations. See the **Transforming variables** chapter for more information about these functions. *

* e.g. Let x = AVG(VARNAME, VARNAME ...)
just separate the variables to be operated on with a comma.

IF...THEN

With the IF...THEN statement, you can execute statements conditionally. The syntax for an IF...THEN statement is:

```
IF condition  THEN  statement
```

The statement that follows THEN can be any legal **DATA** BASIC statement including LET, FOR...NEXT, DELETE, GOTO, and another IF...THEN. Examples of IF...THEN statements are:

```
IF X=99 THEN LET X=.
IF X<20 THEN DELETE
IF CARDIO>400 THEN GOTO 100
IF CARDIO>400 AND CANCER>100 THEN LET RATE$='EXTREME'
IF 2+2 THEN STOP
```

The statement following the THEN is executed only if the condition following the IF is nonzero (not FALSE). Notice that the condition following the IF in the last example (2+2) is nonzero, so the whole statement is equivalent to a STOP statement alone.

You may execute more than one conditional transformation per RUN. If you are testing consecutive IF...THEN conditions on the same variable or variables, you should use IF...THEN...ELSE, discussed below.

ELSE

The examples above tested cases for one condition (e.g., CARDIO>400, or CARDIO>400 AND CANCER>100). If the case met the condition, SYSTAT executed the transformation. If the case did not meet the condition, SYSTAT did not execute the transformation.

You may want, however, to execute many conditional transformations at once. If you are testing consecutive related conditions on the same variable, SYSTAT provides an ELSE statement to accompany IF...THEN.

In their simplest form, IF...THEN and ELSE take the format:

```
IF expression THEN statement
ELSE statement
```

SYSTAT executes the statement following ELSE only when the preceding IF condition evaluates to false. Another IF...THEN statement can follow ELSE, enabling you to string together a number of related conditional transformations:


```
IF expression THEN LET var=expression
ELSE IF expression THEN LET var=expression
ELSE IF expression THEN LET var=expression
ELSE LET var=expression
```

In this case, SYSTAT executes the statement following ELSE only when *all* preceding IF conditions are false. When a preceding condition is true, SYSTAT ignores subsequent ELSE statements.

7.1 Using IF...THEN...ELSE to simplify a program

Here we compare two transformation programs. The first uses only IF...THEN statements to assign values to a new variable called RATE$ based on values for CARDIO:

```
USE USDATA
SAVE NEWDATA
  IF CARDIO<400 THEN LET RATE$='LOW'
  IF CARDIO>=400 AND CARDIO<465,
      THEN LET RATE$='AVERAGE'
  IF CARDIO>=465 THEN LET RATE$='HIGH'
RUN
```

Using IF...THEN and ELSE makes the program simpler and more efficient:

```
USE USDATA
SAVE NEWDATA
  IF CARDIO<400 THEN LET RATE$='LOW'
  ELSE IF CARDIO<465 THEN LET RATE$='AVERAGE'
  ELSE LET RATE$='HIGH'
RUN
```

SYSTAT executes this program once for each case. The order of the IF and ELSE statements is important. The ELSE depends on the truth of the IF conditions before it. SYSTAT executes an ELSE statement only if all preceding conditions are false.

After running this program, check the values for the first 10 cases for CARDIO and RATE$:

```
USE NEWDATA
REPEAT 10
LIST CARDIO, RATE$
RUN
```

```
                         CARDIO         RATE$

Case     1              466.200          HIGH
Case     2              395.900           LOW
Case     3              433.100       AVERAGE
Case     4              460.600       AVERAGE
Case     5              474.100          HIGH
Case     6              423.800       AVERAGE
Case     7              499.500          HIGH
Case     8              464.700       AVERAGE
Case     9              508.700          HIGH
Case    10              443.100       AVERAGE
```

FOR...NEXT

The syntax for a FOR...NEXT statement is:

```
FOR [index=n1 TO n2 [STEP=n3]]
statement
statement
  ...
NEXT
```

Here are some examples:

```
FOR
  LET X=1
  LET Y=2
NEXT

FOR I=1 TO 10
  PRINT I
NEXT

FOR W=0 TO CARDIO<400 STEP URN
  PRINT W
NEXT
```

FOR...NEXT loops are executed for each case (or number of times specified in a REPEAT statement). In the first example above, the FOR...NEXT is superfluous, since the two LET statements are executed only once for each case anyway. In the second example, the PRINT statement is executed 10 times for each case.

The third example is bizarre, but illustrates some important points. First of all, notice that the indices (*n1*,*n2*,*n3*) can be expressions. If CARDIO is greater than or equal to 400 for a case, then W is printed only once (as zero), because the index W runs from zero to zero. Otherwise, W runs from zero to one in increments determined by a uniform random number chosen once before the loop is executed. This means that the PRINT statement will be executed a random number of times for each case where CARDIO is less than 400. This type of construct can be useful in Monte Carlo simulation.

Control

FOR...NEXT loops without an *index* are executed once. Otherwise, FOR...NEXT loops are tested at the beginning to determine whether they should be executed for the current value of *index*. See Example 7.6 for an explicit parsing of a FOR...NEXT loop using GOTO statements. Some other languages may execute FOR...NEXT loops once even when a condition is false. The following example will not print anything:

```
FOR I=6 TO 3 STEP 1
  PRINT I
NEXT
```

Nesting

You can nest up to ten FOR...NEXT loops in this version of SYSTAT. In versions before 4.0, nesting was not allowed.

```
FOR
  FOR
    FOR
      ...
    NEXT
  NEXT
NEXT
```

You must always match every FOR with a NEXT.

7.2 Conditional FOR...NEXT

The mean value for the variable PULMONAR from the data set USDATA is approximately 26.4 with a standard deviation of 5.6. Suppose you want to set RATE$ to "HIGH" and RATE to 1 everywhere that PULMONAR is more than one standard deviation above average.

```
USE USDATA
SAVE NEWDATA
  IF PULMONAR>32 THEN FOR
    LET RATE$='HIGH'
    LET RATE=1
  NEXT
LIST PULMONAR, RATE$, RATE
RUN
```

Here are the first 10 cases output:

```
                      PULMONAR        RATE$       RATE

Case     1              33.600          HIGH        1.000
Case     2              29.600                        .
Case     3              33.100          HIGH        1.000
Case     4              24.900                        .
Case     5              27.400                        .
Case     6              23.200                        .
Case     7              23.900                        .
Case     8              23.300                        .
Case     9              27.000                        .
Case    10              27.400                        .
```

For the cases that meet the condition PULMONAR>32, SYSTAT executes the two transformations between FOR and NEXT. For those cases that do not meet the condition, SYSTAT assigns missing values to RATE$ and RATE.

7.3 FOR...NEXT with ELSE

This example shows the IF...THEN...ELSE format with the FOR...NEXT statement. Suppose you want to make the following assignments:

Where PULMONAR is	*LET RATE$ =*	*Let RATE =*
<20.8	LOW	1
>=20.8 and <32.0	MID	2
>=32.0	HIGH	3

The following program does this:

```
USE USDATA
SAVE NEWDATA
IF PULMONAR<20.8 THEN FOR
   LET RATE$='LOW'
   LET RATE=1
NEXT
ELSE IF PULMONAR<32.0 THEN FOR
   LET RATE$='MID'
   LET RATE=2
NEXT
ELSE FOR
   LET RATE$='HIGH'
   LET RATE=3
NEXT
LIST PULMONAR, RATE$, RATE
RUN
```

The first 10 cases output are:

	PULMONAR	RATE$	RATE
Case 1	33.600	HIGH	3.000
Case 2	29.600	MID	2.000
Case 3	33.100	HIGH	3.000
Case 4	24.900	MID	2.000
Case 5	27.400	MID	2.000
Case 6	23.200	MID	2.000
Case 7	23.900	MID	2.000
Case 8	23.300	MID	2.000
Case 9	27.000	MID	2.000
Case 10	27.400	MID	2.000

If, for a case, PULMONAR is less than 20.8, SYSTAT executes the associated FOR...NEXT statements, setting the values of RATE$ to LOW and RATE to 1. It does not execute the subsequent ELSE statements but moves on to the next case.

If PULMONAR is greater than or equal to 20.8 but less than 32.0, SYSTAT executes the first ELSE statement. SYSTAT sets RATE$ to MID and RATE to 2 and does not execute the second ELSE statement.

If PULMONAR is greater than 32.0, SYSTAT executes the last ELSE statement and sets RATE$ to HIGH and RATE to 3.

FOR...NEXT loops with subscripted variables

You can use FOR...NEXT to define program loops that assign incremental values to an index variable. You can use such a loop to transform a set of subscripted variables. SYSTAT executes the statements between the FOR and the NEXT statements for each successive value of the index variable you specify. The index variable begins with the initial value you assign, does the transformations, and then increases by one. The cycle repeats until the index variable reaches the limit specified with TO.

Examples:

```
FOR I=1 TO 5
FOR TRIAL=1 TO LAST
FOR J=2 TO 20 STEP 2
```

The STEP option adjusts the size of the increment. If you enter the following, SYSTAT increments N by two each time. Its values are therefore 1, 3, 5, 7, and 9 consecutively.

```
FOR N=1 TO 10 STEP 2
```

With this specification, SYSTAT runs through the loop only six times.

Note: if you want to execute a set of commands on a certain number of cases, use the REPEAT command (see REPEAT in this chapter) rather than the FOR...NEXT construct. Remember, every program is executed once for each case. Therefore, if you use FOR...NEXT, **DATA** runs through the loop for every case.

Temporary subscripts using the ARRAY statement

If your variable names are not already subscripted, you can use the ARRAY statement before your BASIC program to assign subscripts temporarily for the purpose of doing transformations inside a FOR...NEXT loop. See the **Programming examples** chapter for more information.

7.4 Logging ten variables

Suppose you have a file containing the variables X(1-10) and you want to calculate the natural log of each. You could either enter ten separate LET commands or use the FOR...NEXT looping construct to do this, e.g.:

```
FOR N=1 TO 10
  LET X(N) = LOG(X(N))
NEXT
```

SYSTAT runs through the loop ten times, increasing the value of N by one each time. Thus, N successively has the values 1, 2, 3, 4, 5, 6, 7, 8, 9, and 10. Therefore, this program is the same as:

```
LET X(1)=LOG(X(1))
LET X(2)=LOG(X(2))
LET X(3)=LOG(X(3))
LET X(4)=LOG(X(4))
LET X(5)=LOG(X(5))
LET X(6)=LOG(X(6))
LET X(7)=LOG(X(7))
LET X(8)=LOG(X(8))
LET X(9)=LOG(X(9))
LET X(10)=LOG(X(10))
```

If you don't want to clobber the values in X by replacing them with their logs, you can assign the transformed values to a new variable Y. See the DIM statement below for how to create a new subscripted variable.

The STEP option adjusts the size of the increment. The following increases N by two each time to values 1, 3, 5, 7, and 9 successively. SYSTAT runs through the loop only five times.

```
FOR N=1 TO 10 STEP 2
```

Therefore, this program is the same as:

```
LET X(1)=LOG(X(1))
LET X(3)=LOG(X(3))
LET X(5)=LOG(X(5))
LET X(7)=LOG(X(7))
LET X(9)=LOG(X(9))
```

DIM

To add new subscripted variables to a file, you must use the DIM statement first. DIM reserves space for new subscripted variables.

For example, the following DIM statement creates new variables X(1), X(2), X(3), X(4), and X(5).

```
DIM X(5)
```

You can use subscripted variables defined with DIM in transformations. Suppose you have variables X(1–10). The following program creates new variables Y(1–10) whose values are the natural logarithms of corresponding values in X(1–10).

```
DIM Y(10)
FOR N=1 TO 10
  LET Y(N) = LOG(X(N))
NEXT
```

Without the DIM statement, SYSTAT would not understand the Y variable subscript in the LET statement and would respond with an error message.

You cannot redimension existing or previously defined arrays of subscripted variables. You can add new variables to an existing array by entering them in the Data Editor, but you cannot do it in **DATA**.

GOTO

A GOTO statement jumps from the current statement to the numbered statement specified. It works only with numbered statements.

For example, GOTO 10 makes **DATA** jump to statement 10. You can combine GOTO with IF...THEN for programming flexibility, e.g.:

```
IF CASE=10 THEN GOTO 50
IF GROUP>3 THEN GOTO 100
```

7.5
Simple GOTO

Here is a simple **DATA** BASIC program using GOTO:

```
10 LET I=J-L
20 LET I=I+L
30  IF I>K THEN GOTO 60
40  PRINT I
50 GOTO 20
60 STOP
```

It is equivalent to the following program that uses the FOR...NEXT construct:

```
10 FOR I=J TO K STEP L
40  PRINT I
50 NEXT
60 STOP
```

You can use IF...THEN with GOTO to program loops like those provided by other languages such as Pascal or FORTRAN. For example, you could program REPEAT...UNTIL, WHILE, or other flow-of-control constructions that **DATA** BASIC does not directly provide.

PRINT

The PRINT command prints the values of variables you specify. You can also use PRINT to print character strings, which is often useful for BASIC programs.

Suppose you have a program that sums the values of a variable. Also suppose that instead of recording the answer (sum) somewhere in the worksheet, you just want the program to display its results. You can do this by issuing a PRINT statement:

```
PRINT "The sum of values in A is ",SUM
```

Such a program is presented as Example 10.16. Note how a PRINT statement lists the text literally (enclosed in quotation marks) and then lists the variable SUM after a comma.

```
USE USDATA
HOLD
IF WINE<>. THEN LET WINESUM=WINESUM+WINE
IF EOF THEN PRINT "Sum of Wine =",WINESUM
RUN
```

As discussed in the **Entering data** chapter, **DATA** prints numeric and character values in 12-column, right-justified fields. Blanks pad the left of each field. Character strings that you specify literally (i.e., not those that are values of character variables you listed in the PRINT command) are not justified; they are printed exactly the way you specified them, but without the surrounding quotation marks.

STOP

The STOP command halts work on the current observation and clears memory for work on the next observation. You will rarely need to use STOP. A possible case where you might want STOP is to terminate a loop when a certain value is reached.

An example using STOP is Example 10.6.

Using REPEAT

For any BASIC program, you can use the REPEAT command to limit the action of the program to a certain number of cases—just as you can use REPEAT 10 to limit the action of commands like LIST to the first ten cases, for instance.

Thus, you can use REPEAT to test complex BASIC programs. If you use REPEAT before RUN, you can see whether the program is correct or if you need to change it before running it on an entire file. For example:

```
REPEAT 3
USE MYFILE
SAVE TESTFILE
LET X=LOG(X)
LET Y=LOG(Y)
SORT
RUN
```

If you made a mistake writing the program, you would find it before wasting your time running the program on the entire file. For files with several hundred cases, a brief trial run can pay off. After you are sure everything is OK, type REPEAT with no arguments to restore the counter.

Computation

Numerical accuracy

DATA BASIC was designed specifically for statistical and scientific computation. All arithmetic is done in double precision using algorithms chosen for their accuracy. Therefore, **DATA** BASIC is usually more accurate than other implementations of the BASIC programming language. For example, if you type the following commands:

```
REPEAT 1
LET X = INT(2.6*7-0.2)
PRINT X
RUN
```

SYSTAT prints the correct value, 18.000, and reports that one case and one variable were processed. This is the correct answer. Some BASICs return an incorrect value of 17. You might want to try this in your own computer's version of BASIC. If it returns an incorrect value, do not trust any programs written in that language.

Memory limitations

You can run out of memory if your program is too long. If you get an out of memory error message, reduce the number of transformations that you execute in a single run.

8 Sorting, ranking, and standardizing

Sorting, ranking, and standardizing 8

Overview

This chapter shows you how to sort, rank, and standardize data in SYSTAT.

RANK *varlist*	Transforms all numeric variables in *varlist* to ranks. Each variable is ranked within its own distribution. The default is all numeric variables in the file.
SORT *varlist*	Sorts the datafile on the variables specified in *varlist*. *Varlist* can include numeric or character variables or both. The default is all variables in the file, in the order that they appear in the file.
STANDARDIZE *varlist*	Standardizes the numeric variables named in *varlist*. The default is all numeric variables in the file.

Sorting

The SORT command sorts a file in ascending order by up to ten numeric and/or character variables.

Examples are:

```
SORT
SORT AGE
SORT NAME$
SORT SEX$, AGE
```

If you do not specify any variables in the SORT command, as in the first example, SYSTAT sorts using the first variable in the file. The last example shows a nested sort. SYSTAT would sort this file first by SEX$ and then by AGE within SEX$.

Sorting orders cases in increasing numerical order. Missing values come first. SYSTAT sorts character data in ascending ASCII order, with blanks (missing values) at the beginning. The sequence for an ascending character sort is:

33–39				!	"	#	$	%	&	'
40–49	(	)	*	+	,	-	.	/	0	1
50–59	2	3	4	5	6	7	8	9	:	;
60–69	<	=	>	?	@	A	B	C	D	E
70–79	F	G	H	I	J	K	L	M	N	O
80–89	P	Q	R	S	T	U	V	W	X	Y
90–99	Z	[	\	]	^	_	`	a	b	c
100–09	d	e	f	g	h	i	j	k	l	m
110–19	n	o	p	q	r	s	t	u	v	w
120–26	x	y	z	{	|	}	~			

This means that words are sorted alphabetically with upper-case words preceding lower case. (Note that if you sort a character variable containing numeric values, those values are sorted from left to right, rather than small to big: 1, 12, 150, 2, 31, 4000, 5.4, etc.)

If you want to retain the data in their sorted order, you *must* save them to a new file. Sorting, by itself, does not create a sorted permanent file.

Enter the following data to use in the examples:

```
SAVE TEMP
INPUT SEX$, AGE
LET N=Case
RUN
FEMALE 5
MALE 6
MALE 4
FEMALE 6
FEMALE 5
MALE 6
MALE 8
FEMALE 3
MALE 6
FEMALE 5
MALE 4
MALE 5
FEMALE 5
FEMALE 6
~
```

The variable N stores the original case number, so each case includes a value for SEX$, AGE, and its index.

8.1 Simple sort

The following program sorts the file TEMP on the variable SEX$.

```
USE TEMP
SAVE SORT1
SORT SEX$
RUN
```

SYSTAT reports on its progress.

```
Begin sort
    14 cases sorted
Saving sorted file
End sort
```

Now list the file.

```
USE SORT1
LIST
RUN
```

```
                          SEX$        AGE          N

Case      1              FEMALE      5.000       1.000
Case      2              FEMALE      6.000       4.000
Case      3              FEMALE      5.000       5.000
Case      4              FEMALE      3.000       8.000
Case      5              FEMALE      5.000      10.000
Case      6              FEMALE      5.000      13.000
Case      7              FEMALE      6.000      14.000
Case      8                MALE      6.000       2.000
Case      9                MALE      4.000       3.000
Case     10                MALE      6.000       6.000
Case     11                MALE      8.000       7.000
Case     12                MALE      6.000       9.000
Case     13                MALE      4.000      11.000
Case     14                MALE      5.000      12.000
```

SYSTAT has rearranged the file so that the cases where SEX$ equals "FEMALE" come before those where SEX$ equals "MALE." (Remember that N represents the original position of each case in the file.)

This program sorts the file by AGE:

```
USE TEMP
SAVE SORT2
SORT AGE
RUN
```

Here are the cases in the new file SORT2.

		SEX$	AGE	N
Case	1	FEMALE	3.000	8.000
Case	2	MALE	4.000	3.000
Case	3	MALE	4.000	11.000
Case	4	FEMALE	5.000	1.000
Case	5	FEMALE	5.000	5.000
Case	6	FEMALE	5.000	10.000
Case	7	MALE	5.000	12.000
Case	8	FEMALE	5.000	13.000
Case	9	MALE	6.000	2.000
Case	10	FEMALE	6.000	4.000
Case	11	MALE	6.000	6.000
Case	12	MALE	6.000	9.000
Case	13	FEMALE	6.000	14.000
Case	14	MALE	8.000	7.000

In this example, SYSTAT has rearranged the cases so that the values of AGE go from smallest to largest down the file.

8.2
Nested sort

This example illustrates a nested sort. The program first sorts on the variable SEX$. Then, within SEX$, it sorts the cases based on AGE.

```
USE TEMP
SAVE SORT3
SORT SEX$, AGE
RUN
```

A LIST of the file SORT3 produces:

		SEX$	AGE	N
Case	1	FEMALE	3.000	8.000
Case	2	FEMALE	5.000	1.000
Case	3	FEMALE	5.000	5.000
Case	4	FEMALE	5.000	10.000
Case	5	FEMALE	5.000	13.000
Case	6	FEMALE	6.000	4.000
Case	7	FEMALE	6.000	14.000
Case	8	MALE	4.000	3.000
Case	9	MALE	4.000	11.000
Case	10	MALE	5.000	12.000
Case	11	MALE	6.000	2.000
Case	12	MALE	6.000	6.000
Case	13	MALE	6.000	9.000
Case	14	MALE	8.000	7.000

Notice again, that SYSTAT arranges the file so that cases where SEX$ equals "FEMALE" come before those where SEX$ equals "MALE." Within each of these groups, SYSTAT now arranges the cases so that the values for AGE go from smallest to largest. This is a nested sort.

8.3 Computing medians

You can get medians with the STEM command in **SYGRAPH**. Here is a **DATA** program for computing medians.

The program has three steps. First, it sorts the file on the variable for which you want to find the median. Next, the program creates the variables N, N1, and N2. N is the total number of cases. If the number of cases is odd, N1 and N2 are both the case number of the middle case. If the number of cases is even, N1 and N2 are the case numbers of the two middle cases. The HOLD command keeps the final values of these variables in memory for use in the third step. Finally, the program computes the median value.

Here we find the median of CARDIO:

```
USE USDATA
SAVE SORTDATA
SORT CARDIO
RUN

USE SORTDATA
HOLD
LET N=CASE
LET N1=INT(N/2)+1
LET N2=N-N1+1
RUN

IF CASE=N1 THEN LET MEDIAN=MEDIAN+CARDIO/2
IF CASE=N2 THEN LET MEDIAN=MEDIAN+CARDIO/2
IF EOF THEN PRINT "The median of CARDIO is",MEDIAN
RUN
```

```
The median value of CARDIO is          416.200

   50 Cases and    47 variables processed.
No SYSTAT file created.
```

The EOF variable is used to mark "End Of File." See the **Subgroup processing** chapter for more information on this system variable.

You can find the median of a variable in a small to medium-sized file with the STEM or BOX commands in **SYGRAPH**. This **DATA** program is not limited by internal memory, so it can find the median for any number of cases.

8.4
Computing quantiles

The following program prints the quantiles of a variable:

```
USE RAWDATA
SAVE SORTDATA
SORT X
RUN
USE SORTDATA
HOLD
LET N=CASE
RUN
LET Q=CASE/(N+1)
LIST X,Q
RUN
```

Ranking

The RANK command ranks variables.

Examples are:

```
RANK
RANK RAINFALL
RANK JUDGEMENT, SCORE
```

The first example ranks all the numeric variables in the file. When SYSTAT ranks a variable, it replaces the original values with their ranks. If two or more values are the same, SYSTAT averages their ranks.

8.5
Simple ranks

This example uses the data file TEMP created in the previous section. It creates a variable AGERANK which contains the rank values of AGE.

```
USE TEMP
SAVE RANKDATA
LET AGERANK=AGE
RANK AGERANK
RUN
```



```
   14 Cases and    3 variables processed.
SYSTAT file created.
Please wait while data are processed and resaved.
Begin rank.
End rank.
```

Now list AGE and AGERANK.

```
USE RANKDATA
LIST AGE, AGERANK
RUN
```

		AGE	AGERANK
Case	1	5.000	6.000
Case	2	6.000	11.000
Case	3	4.000	2.500
Case	4	6.000	11.000
Case	5	5.000	6.000
Case	6	6.000	11.000
Case	7	8.000	14.000
Case	8	3.000	1.000
Case	9	6.000	11.000
Case	10	5.000	6.000
Case	11	4.000	2.500
Case	12	5.000	6.000
Case	13	5.000	6.000
Case	14	6.000	11.000

This shows that case 8 has the lowest value of AGE, cases 3 and 11 share the next lowest values, and so on up to case 7, which has the greatest value.

Here we show AGE and AGERANK from the sorted file. Note that ranks are simply the case numbers of the sorted file, with ties averaged.

		AGE	AGERANK
Case	1	3.000	1.000
Case	2	4.000	2.500
Case	3	4.000	2.500
Case	4	5.000	6.000
Case	5	5.000	6.000
Case	6	5.000	6.000
Case	7	5.000	6.000
Case	8	5.000	6.000
Case	9	6.000	11.000
Case	10	6.000	11.000
Case	11	6.000	11.000
Case	12	6.000	11.000
Case	13	6.000	11.000
Case	14	8.000	14.000

8.6 Ranking large files

The RANK command does its work in memory. Therefore, you can run out of room with files containing thousands of cases. If this happens, first SORT the file by the variable you wish to rank. Then, replace the values of the rank variable with the case number. The following program again ranks the variable AGE:

```
USE TEMP
LET AGERANK=AGE
SORT AGERANK
RUN
LET AGERANK=CASE
SAVE RANKDAT2
LIST AGE,AGERANK
RUN
```

Note that in this example the data do not remain in the original order. Preserving that order requires a more complicated program:

```
USE TEMP
LET ORIGINAL=CASE
LET AGERANK=AGE
SORT AGERANK
RUN
LET AGERANK=CASE
SORT ORIGINAL
SAVE RANKDAT3
DROP ORIGINAL
RUN
```

Neither program is capable of averaging tied ranks. (That task is left as an exercise for the reader.)

8.7 Winsorized and trimmed means

To "ten percent trim" a variable, rank the variable and then DELETE the upper and lower ten percent of the data values. You can then compute a ten percent trimmed mean of the variable with the STATISTICS command from **STATS**. This example computes a ten percent trim for the variable X from a data file called RAWDATA:

The first part of the program makes a copy of X that we then use for ranking.


```
USE RAWDATA
LET RX=X
RANK RX
RUN
```

The next part finds the number of cases in the file. We use HOLD to keep the last value of N for the final part of the program.

```
HOLD
LET N=CASE
RUN
```

The final part deletes the extreme observations.

```
SAVE RAWDATA
IF RX<N/10 OR RX>9*N/10 THEN DELETE
RUN
```

Programs similar to the trimmed means program can Winsorize means, biweight cases, and weight cases with various schemes through use of the RANK function. See Barnett and Lewis (1978), Launer and Wilkinson (1979), and Huber (1977) for more information on these procedures. You can also use fractional ranks in formulas to compute trimmed means, if you wish.

8.8 Normalized scores

A normalized score is the standard normal deviate corresponding to the sample quantile of an observed value. It can be thought of in two ways: as the z-score the value would have if the observed distribution were perfectly normal, or as the distance of the value from the mean in standard units. In any case, do not confuse normalized scores, which necessarily have a perfect normal distribution, with z scores, which do not. (See "Standardizing" below for how to produce z scores.)

Converting scores to normal scores reshapes the observed distribution into a normal distribution. In practice, the effectiveness of this procedure is limited by the number of distinct values and their distribution in the original sample. There are limits to how normal one can make binary data! Some nonparametric tests are equivalent to performing parametric tests (t-tests, ANOVA, etc.) on normalized values of dependent variables.

The following is similar to the program we used to produce trimmed means. It saves normalized scores for X (XNORM) back into the file.

The first part makes a copy of X that we then use for ranking.

```
USE RAWDATA
LET RX=X
RANK RX
RUN
```

The next part finds the number of cases in the file. We use HOLD because we need to use the final value of N in the next step.

```
HOLD
LET N=CASE
RUN
```

The final part takes the inverse normal density function of the sample quantiles. See the **Transforming variables** chapter for information about ZIF (Z inverse function).

```
SAVE RAWDATA
LET XNORM = ZIF(RX/(N+1))
DROP RX,N
RUN
```

Standardizing

You can standardize one or more variables in **DATA** with the STANDARDIZE command. STANDARDIZE replaces values of variables with their sample standard scores, or *z*-scores.

Examples are:

```
STANDARDIZE
STANDARDIZE QUESTION(1-5)
```

8.9 Standardizing ages

This example uses the data set TEMP we created before Example 8.1 at the beginning of this chapter. The example creates and lists a variable AGESTAND that contains the standardized values of AGE.

```
USE TEMP
SAVE STANDATA
LET AGESTAND=AGE
STANDARDIZE AGESTAND
RUN
USE STANDATA
LIST AGE, AGESTAND
RUN
```

```
   14 Cases and    4 variables processed.
SYSTAT file created.
Please wait while data are processed and resaved.
Begin standardize
End standardize

                        AGE     AGESTAND

 Case      1            5.000       -0.237
 Case      2            6.000        0.593
 Case      3            4.000       -1.068
 Case      4            6.000        0.593
 Case      5            5.000       -0.237
 Case      6            6.000        0.593
 Case      7            8.000        2.254
 Case      8            3.000       -1.898
 Case      9            6.000        0.593
 Case     10            5.000       -0.237
 Case     11            4.000       -1.068
 Case     12            5.000       -0.237
 Case     13            5.000       -0.237
 Case     14            6.000        0.593
```

AGESTAND now has standardized AGE values, with mean 0 and standard deviation 1. Remember that standardizing does not change the shape of your data. If the data are highly skewed or bimodal before standardizing, they will be so after. Standardizing simply moves the location and spread of your values.

9 Subgroup processing

Subgroup processing 9

Overview

This chapter shows how to process subgroups of data using **DATA**'s built-in variables BOF (Beginning Of File), EOF (End Of File), BOG (Beginning Of Group), and EOG (End Of Group).

Note that, to pick out only one subgroup in **DATA**, you can use either IF...THEN or DELETE. Furthermore, every statistical module has BY and SELECT to create temporary subgroups.

BY *varlist*	Activates the two system variables BOG and EOG (Beginning Of Group and End Of Group).

Built-in grouping variables

You can write programs that operate on subgroups of cases in a file. To do this, you must first specify variables in your file that define subgroups. **DATA** has four special grouping variables that are always available for processing subgroups:

BOF has value 1 if beginning-of-file, else it is 0
EOF has value 1 if end-of-file, else it is 0
BOG has value 1 if beginning-of-BY group, else it is 0
EOG has value 1 if end-of-BY group, else it is 0

The BY statement identifies the variables that define subgroups with BOG and EOG in your data. You may name up to 10 variables in a BY statement. You *must* sort your file by these variables. To clear a previous BY command, type BY with no arguments.

You may use BOG, EOG, BOF, and EOF within conditional expressions in IF...THEN statements. For example, the statement:

```
IF BOG THEN statement
```

causes SYSTAT to execute *statement* every time it encounters a new value in a BY variable. This is because the value of BOG is 1 ("true") for every case that begins a new group, and 0 otherwise.

9.1
Printing the last case in a file

The following procedure prints the value of CARDIO for the last case in the USDATA file. EOF is 0 for every case but the last, where its value is 1.

```
USE USDATA
IF EOF THEN PRINT,
   "The CARDIO value for the last case is",CARDIO
RUN
```

To print all but the last case, you can set the condition to one of the following:

```
IF EOF=0 THEN …
IF NOT EOF THEN …
```

9.2 Computing subgroup means

The data set USDATA is sorted on the variable REGION. There are four regions and therefore four BY groups. This program calculates the mean of the variable SPIRITS for each region. The HOLD command enables the program to sum across cases. On the last case for each group, SYSTAT calculates and prints the mean, then resets SUM and N to 0.

```
USE USDATA
BY REGION
HOLD
 LET N=N+1
 LET SUM=SUM+SPIRITS
 IF EOG THEN FOR
   LET MEAN=SUM/N
   PRINT "The mean spirits consumption rate"
   PRINT " for Region",REGION," is",MEAN
   LET SUM=0
   LET N=0
 NEXT
RUN
```

```
The mean spirits consumption rate
  for Region          1.000  is                   3.149
The mean spirits consumption rate
  for Region          2.000  is                   2.203
The mean spirits consumption rate
  for Region          3.000  is                   2.256
The mean spirits consumption rate
  for Region          4.000  is                   2.785

   50 cases and   46 variables processed.
SYSTAT file created.
```

10 Programming examples

Programming examples 10

Overview

The examples in this chapter show more applications of **DATA** BASIC, including statistical calculations and data management procedures. There are simpler ways to accomplish many of these tasks, particularly generating random numbers, but the programs in this chapter were selected to illustrate the full range of **DATA** BASIC capabilities.

The chapter also introduces the HOLD command, which retains variables in memory for successive operations. HOLD enables you to do sums and counts of your data across cases, create lag variables, and execute complex data transformations.

ARRAY *array / varlist*	Aliases the variables in *varlist* to an array of subscripted variables. The variables have the root name *array* with integer subscripts 1 through *n*, where *n* is the number of variables in *varlist*. Note that ARRAY works differently in versions prior to 3.2. See Example 10.2 for demonstration.
HOLD	Initializes all numeric values in a BASIC program to zero and retains numeric values from one case to the next. HOLD stays in effect until you QUIT the program, type NEW, or USE another file.
RSEED=#	Specifies the random number seed #. The default is 313. You can specify any integer between 1 and 30,000.

Operations within rows

The following examples show you how to use the array capabilities in **DATA** BASIC to perform operations within rows (cases) of a dataset.

10.1 Computing means of subscripted variables

The following program computes the average of the variables X(1) through X(10) for each case. The program checks for missing data. You can calculate the mean more easily with the multi-variable function AVG.

```
USE MYDATA
SAVE NEWDATA
LET SUMX=0
LET N=0
FOR I=1 TO 10
   IF X(I)<>. THEN FOR
      LET SUMX=SUMX+X(I)
      LET N=N+1
   NEXT
NEXT
IF N<>0 THEN LET MEAN=SUMX/N
ELSE LET MEAN=.
RUN
```

Like all BASIC programs, the program runs once for each case.

At the start of each case, LET SUMX=0 and LET N=0 set the variables SUMX and N to zero. SUMX sums the non-missing values across each case, and N counts the non-missing values for each case.

The FOR...NEXT loop runs the variables X(1–10) through two conditional transformations. In the first, if X(I) is not missing, its value is added to SUMX. In the second, again if X(I) is not missing, the count variable N is increased by one.

Upon completion of the FOR...NEXT loop, another conditional transformation tests whether N is not equal to zero. If N is not equal to zero, then the calculation MEAN=SUMX/N is executed. If N equals zero (because the values of X(1–10) for the current case are all missing), dividing by N would cause an error. Therefore, SYSTAT executes the ensuing ELSE statement and sets MEAN to missing (.).

10.2 Computing means of unsubscripted variables

To average variables that are not subscripted, use the ARRAY command to alias the variables with a subscripted variable and then use the same logic as above. The example below averages the values of the liquor consumption variables in the data set USDATA. Although USDATA has no missing values, the program tests for them anyway.

```
USE USDATA
SAVE NEWDATA
ARRAY LIQUOR/SPIRITS,WINE,BEER
LET SUMALCOH=0
LET N=0
FOR I=1 TO 3
   IF LIQUOR(I)<>. THEN FOR
      LET SUMALCOH=SUMALCOH+LIQUOR(I)
      LET N=N+1
   NEXT
NEXT
IF N<>0 THEN LET MEAN=SUMALCOH/N
ELSE LET MEAN=.
RUN
```

SYSTAT treats each variable specified in the ARRAY statement as an element in a subscripted variable named LIQUOR.

SPIRITS ≡ LIQUOR(1)
WINE ≡ LIQUOR(2)
BEER ≡ LIQUOR(3)

Generating random numbers

SYSTAT contains many built-in random number generators. These can generate random numbers with a uniform distribution, standard normal distribution, *t* distribution, *F* distribution, chi-square distribution, Beta distribution, or Gamma distribution. See the **Transforming variables** chapter for the names of these functions.

Use the built-in function URN to obtain uniformly distributed random numbers. SYSTAT generates uniform random numbers between zero and one by a triple modulo method. Each uniform is constructed from three multiplicative congruential generators with prime modulus. The initial seeds for each generator are 13579, 12345, and 313 (Wichmann and Hill, 1982). You may reset the last random number seed by using the RSEED command, where # is an integer between 1 and 30,000.

```
RSEED=#
```

Use the built-in variable ZRN to obtain normally distributed random numbers. ZRN generates pseudo-random standard normal variates with a mean of 0 and a standard deviation of 1. SYSTAT generates normal random numbers from uniforms by applying the inverse normal cumulative distribution function to uniform variates between 0 and 1.

The following examples use **DATA** BASIC to generate random numbers for a variety of distributions using only the uniform and normal generators. Each example demonstrates how to generate a sample from a different type of random distribution.

The REPEAT 100 command in each program tells SYSTAT to create 100 cases. Change this value to vary the number of cases in the generated samples.

10.3 Uniform distribution on (0,1)

This program creates a variable X that contains uniform random numbers between 0 and 1.

```
SAVE URANDOM
REPEAT 100
LET X=URN
RUN
```

10.4 Uniform distribution on (a,b)

This program generates a variable U that contains uniform random numbers between A and B.

```
SAVE URANDOM
REPEAT 100
LET A=0
LET B=10
LET U=A+(B-A)*URN
DROP A,B
RUN
```

10.5 Uniform integers

This program generates a variable I that contains uniform random integers between and including A and B.

```
SAVE IRANDOM
REPEAT 100
LET A=1
LET B=9
LET I=A+INT(URN*(B-A+1))
DROP A,B
RUN
```

10.6 Normal distribution using URN

Using uniform random numbers, this program creates a variable X that contains random numbers with a mean of 0 and a standard deviation of 1. It uses a modification of the Box-Muller method (Box & Muller, 1958; Marsaglia, 1961; Sibuya, 1962). The built-in function ZRN is, of course, faster. See the next example.

```
SAVE NRANDOM
REPEAT 100
10 LET X = 2*URN - 1
20 LET Y = 2*URN - 1
30 LET XY = X*X+Y*Y
40 IF XY>=1 THEN GOTO 10
50 LET Z = SQR(-2*LOG(XY)/XY)
60 LET NRAN1 = X*Z
70 LET NRAN2 = Y*Z
80 STOP
RUN
```

10.7 Normal distribution using ZRN

This program creates a variable X that contains random numbers with a mean of 0 and a standard deviation of 1. It uses the built-in normal random variate function.

```
SAVE NRANDOM
REPEAT 100
LET X=ZRN
RUN
```

10.8 Normal distribution with specified parameters

This program generates a variable Z that contains normal random numbers with mean MU and standard deviation SIGMA.

```
SAVE ZRANDOM

REPEAT 100
LET MU=value
LET SIGMA=value
LET Z=MU+SIGMA*ZRN
DROP MU,SIGMA
RUN
```

10.9 Chi-square distribution

This program generates a variable CHISQ that contains a chi-square distribution with NDF degrees-of-freedom. The XRN function (see the **Transforming** chapter) is faster.

```
SAVE CRANDOM
REPEAT 100
LET NDF=10
LET CHISQ=0
FOR I=1 TO NDF
  LET CHISQ=CHISQ+ZRN^2
NEXT
DROP NDF
RUN
```

10.10
t **distribution**

This program generates a variable T that contains a *t* distribution with NDF degrees-of-freedom. It does this by taking the ratio of a normal to the square root of a chi-square divided by its degrees-of-freedom. The built-in function TRN is faster.

```
SAVE TRANDOM
REPEAT 100
LET NDF=10
LET CHISQ=0
FOR I=1 TO NDF
  LET CHISQ=CHISQ+ZRN^2
NEXT
LET T=ZRN/SQR(CHISQ/NDF)
DROP NDF,CHISQ
RUN
```

10.11
F **distribution**

This program generates a variable F that contains an *F* distribution with MDF and NDF degrees-of-freedom. It does this by taking the ratio of two chi-squares divided by their degrees-of-freedom. The built-in function FRN is, of course, faster.

```
SAVE FRANDOM
REPEAT 100
LET MDF=2
LET NDF=10
LET CHISQ1=0
LET CHISQ2=0
FOR I=1 TO MDF
  LET CHISQ1=CHISQ1+ZRN^2
NEXT
FOR I=1 TO NDF
  LET CHISQ2=CHISQ2+ZRN^2
NEXT
LET F=(CHISQ1/MDF)/(CHISQ2/NDF)
DROP MDF,NDF,CHISQ1,CHISQ2
RUN
```

10.12
Multinormal random variables

This is how to generate multinormal random variables with known covariance matrix.

1) Input the population covariance matrix with **DATA**, specifying TYPE=COVARIANCE

2) Obtain principal components for the matrix in **FACTOR**.

3) Generate normal random numbers in **DATA** and multiply them by the factor loadings. Here is an example:

```
DATA
INPUT A B C
TYPE COVARIANCE
SAVE COVA
RUN
2
1  3
.5  1.5  4

FACTOR
FACTOR

DATA
REPEAT 1000        (or whatever N you want)
SAVE NORRAN
LET Z1=ZRN
LET Z2=ZRN
LET Z3=ZRN
LET F1= .666 * Z1 + .908 * Z2 + .856 * Z3
LET F2=1.379 * Z1 + .766 * Z2 - .716 * Z3
LET F3=1.742 * Z1 - .953 * Z2 + .240 * Z3
DROP Z1, Z2, Z3
RUN
```

The numbers in the three equations yielding F1–F3 are the "component loadings" printed in the **FACTOR** output. If you have many variables, you may want to use subscripts in the above example. You can use the BY command to generate multiple samples for a simulation.

To check your work, use **CORR** to obtain the covariance matrix of the variables in the generated sample:

```
CORR
USE NORRAN
COVARIANCE
```

Here is the output for our example:

```
Covariance Matrix

        F1       F2       F3

F1   1.911
F2   1.003    3.010
F3    .634    1.535    4.142
```

Notice that these are close, but not exactly equal to the population covariances because this sample is finite (1000).

Selecting random subsamples

The examples below illustrate two methods of taking random samples without replacement from data files. The first extracts a percentage of cases from a file, and the second a specific number of cases.

10.13 Selecting a percentage of cases

To pick a random sample of approximately three-fourths of a file, type:

```
USE USDATA

SAVE NEWDATA
  IF URN>.75 THEN DELETE
RUN
```

To vary the sample size, change the .75 proportion to another number between 0 and 1.

Here is another method which keeps both selected and deselected cases in the same file. The WEIGHT variable can be used with statistical procedures to select the random subsample for cross-validation.

```
USE USDATA
SAVE NEWDATA
  IF URN>.75 THEN LET WEIGHT=0
  ELSE LET WEIGHT=1
RUN
```

10.14 Selecting a specific number of cases

To pick a random sample of an exact size from a file you must use the HOLD command, which is discussed in more detail in the next section. This program uses an algorithm due to Bebbington (1975). You should replace *orig#* with the number of cases in the original file and *sample#* with the number of cases you want in the sample.

```
USE USDATA
SAVE SDATAFIL
HOLD
  IF CASE=1 THEN LET NF=orig#
  IF CASE=1 THEN LET NS=sample#
  LET RAND=URN
  IF RAND>NS/NF THEN DELETE
  ELSE LET NS=NS-1
  LET NF=NF-1
DROP NF, NS, RAND
RUN
```

Using the HOLD command

The HOLD command changes three default settings in SYSTAT.

1) Without HOLD, SYSTAT operates on one observation at a time and then clears out its memory before repeating the program on the next observation (case). With HOLD, SYSTAT holds values in memory from one case to the next.

2) Without HOLD, SYSTAT sets the initial values of new numeric variables to missing (.). With HOLD, new numeric variables have initial values of zero (0).

3) Without HOLD, SYSTAT clears the workspace after it executes a RUN. With HOLD, SYSTAT does not clear the workspace. You can execute another program on the current file without issuing a USE command. Also, SYSTAT holds the values from the last case of the previous operation in memory.

HOLD is useful for tasks where you need to use the results of a previous calculation in a subsequent task. You will need to use HOLD when changing values of a variable by a constant increment, summing one or more variables (columns), summing subgroups, counting subgroups, and performing other complex calculations.

HOLD is not a true BASIC command in that you cannot precede it with a line number. You can, however, use HOLD with any BASIC program.

HOLD stays in effect until you exit **DATA** or use NEW. Keep this in mind if you run several programs during one **DATA** session.

10.15 Incrementing values of a variable

The following program creates variables X and Y; X increases by 3 for each case and Y increases by 1 every five cases. The REPEAT 15 statement tells SYSTAT to execute the operation 15 times, thereby creating 15 cases. Notice that X is initialized as zero the first time through this program because of HOLD.

```
SAVE INCREM
HOLD
REPEAT 15
  LET X = X+3
  LET Y = 1+INT((Case-1)/5)
LIST
RUN
```

		X	Y
Case	1	3.000	1.000
Case	2	6.000	1.000
Case	3	9.000	1.000
Case	4	12.000	1.000
Case	5	15.000	1.000
Case	6	18.000	2.000
Case	7	21.000	2.000
Case	8	24.000	2.000
Case	9	27.000	2.000
Case	10	30.000	2.000
Case	11	33.000	3.000
Case	12	36.000	3.000
Case	13	39.000	3.000
Case	14	42.000	3.000
Case	15	45.000	3.000

Without HOLD, SYSTAT would initialize X to missing. Therefore, all subsequent calculations done with X would result in missing values.

10.16 Summing a variable

The following program prints the sum of the variable WINE from the dataset USDATA.

```
USE USDATA
HOLD
IF WINE<>. THEN LET WINESUM = WINESUM+WINE
IF EOF THEN PRINT "Sum of Wine =",WINESUM
RUN
```

The first transformation includes the condition IF WINE<>. to make sure we do not add a missing value to WINESUM. If we did, WINESUM would become missing as well. The next transformation contains the condition IF EOF. EOF (end-of-file) is a built-in variable that is true if the current case is the last case in the file, but false otherwise.

```
Sum of Wine =          138.980

   50 cases and   44 variables processed.
SYSTAT file created.
```

10.17 Summing a variable for selected cases

The following program prints the sum of the variable WINE for all values of DIVISION greater than 3. It works like the previous example except that it adds another condition to the summation statement:

```
USE USDATA
HOLD
IF DIVISION>3 AND WINE<>. THEN LET WINESUM=WINESUM+WINE
IF EOF THEN,
 PRINT "Sum of Wine for Regions 4 through 9 is",WINESUM
RUN
```

```
Sum of WINE for Divisions 4 through 9 is   91.620

   50 cases and   44 variables processed.
SYSTAT file created.
```

10.18 Counting cases meeting a condition

The following program counts and prints the number of states in the USDATA data set where the average anual consumption of spirits per person is more than three gallons.

This program resembles the one above that sums WINE for cases where REGION is greater than 3. In this program, however, instead of summing a variable, we add 1 to a counting variable COUNT for each case where SPIRITS is greater than 3.

```
USE USDATA
HOLD
IF SPIRITS>3 THEN LET COUNT=COUNT+1
IF EOF THEN PRINT 'COUNT =',COUNT
RUN
```

SYSTAT tells you that you have not saved your work to a file and asks if you want to. If yes, hit Enter. SYSTAT responds:

```
COUNT =              9.000

   50 cases and   44 variables processed.
No SYSTAT file created.
```

10.19 Standardizing a variable

The following program standardizes a variable, taking advantage of all three features of the HOLD command: new variables are initialized to zero, values are held in memory from one case to the next, and the workspace is not cleared after a RUN.

Note: you could standardize data more easily with the STANDARDIZE command in **DATA**. This example merely illustrates HOLD.

Three RUNs execute the procedure. The first creates a data file; the second computes the sum (SUM), sum of squares (SUMSQ), and total number of cases (N); the third rereads the data and standardizes it.

```
NOTE 'This step creates a file of the raw data.'
SAVE RAW
INPUT X
RUN
9999991
9999992
9999993
~

    3 cases and    1 variables processed.
SYSTAT file created.

NOTE 'This step computes sum, sum of squares, and
count.'
USE RAW
HOLD
LET SUM=SUM+X
LET SUMSQ=SUMSQ+X*X
LET N=CASE
LIST X,N
RUN

                          X              N

 Case     1        9999991.000        1.000
 Case     2        9999992.000        2.000
 Case     3        9999993.000        3.000

    3 cases and    4 variables processed.
SYSTAT file created.

NOTE 'This step rereads the data and standardizes.'
SAVE STANDARD
IF CASE=1 THEN FOR
   LET MEAN = SUM/N
   LET SD = SQR((SUMSQ-SUM*MEAN)/(N-1))
NEXT
LET Z = (X-MEAN)/SD
LIST Z
RUN
```

```
                        Z

Case      1           -1.000
Case      2            0.000
Case      3            1.000

   3 cases and    6 variables processed.
SYSTAT file created.
```

Note that HOLD initializes SUM and SUMSQ to zero. If we do not use HOLD, they are initialized to missing (.). Also, because we used HOLD, SYSTAT holds the values for SUM and SUMSQ in memory from one case to the next. Without HOLD, SYSTAT treats the cases independently and cannot execute any summations.

In the third step, we calculate MEAN and SD only for CASE=1 because the same values will be used to standardize all cases. SYSTAT retains their values from the prior RUN because of the HOLD command.

The built-in function STANDARDIZE does the same work more efficiently. This example, however, gives us a chance to point out another feature of SYSTAT. If your data have large means, small standard deviations, and many observations, the "desk calculator" formulas used above can cause round-off errors. Since SYSTAT does its arithmetic in double precision, this should rarely happen. Even with the nasty example above, we can get away with the desk calculator formula because we have at least 15 decimal digits of precision.

Here is a "provisional" algorithm for standardizing. Note that SUMSQ is no longer the total sum of squares. MEAN and SUMSQ accumulate variation about a provisional mean; after the last observation is processed, that variation becomes the actual mean. This algorithm is used in all SYSTAT procedures that require sample moments.

```
SAVE RAW
INPUT X
RUN
9999991
9999992
9999993
~
```



```
USE RAW
HOLD
LET WT = 1-1/CASE
LET XS = X-MEAN
LET MEAN = MEAN+XS/CASE
LET SUMSQ = SUMSQ+WT*XS*XS
LET N = CASE
LIST X,N
RUN

SAVE STANDARD
IF CASE = 1 THEN LET SD=SQR(SUMSQ/(N-1))
LET Z = (X-MEAN)/SD
LIST Z
RUN
```

The HOLD command does not limit SYSTAT to two-pass transformations. Indeed, it is possible to make three or more passes on the same file for smoothing, lagging variables, or other procedures. Remember, however, to try your program on a few cases to debug it before committing it to the entire data file.

10.20 Lagging variables

You can use HOLD to create lagged variables. A lag is a copy of a variable offset by a number of cases. Lags are used in time series and forecasting to see if a variable is auto- or self-correlated. The built-in function LAG does the same operation as the example below. In the following example, LAG is a lag of X offset by one case:

X	LAG
2	.
4	2
6	4
8	6
10	8

First, make a file with X.

```
SAVE FILE1
INPUT X
RUN
2
4
6
8
10
~
```

Now, create LAG.

```
NEW
USE FILE1
SAVE FILE2
HOLD
10 LET LAG=TEMP
15 IF CASE=1 THEN LET LAG=.
20 LET TEMP = X
DROP TEMP
LIST X LAG
RUN
```

```
                          X           LAG

 Case     1              2.000          .
 Case     2              4.000        2.000
 Case     3              6.000        4.000
 Case     4              8.000        6.000
 Case     5             10.000        8.000

    5 cases and     2 variables processed.
SYSTAT file created.
```

Note that the DROP command prevents TEMP from being saved into FILE2.

The program works as follows:

LAG and TEMP are new variables with initial values of 0.

Case 1. The first value of LAG is set to missing. TEMP stores X's value for Case 1, which is 2.

Case 2. Because we are using HOLD, SYSTAT remembers the value for TEMP (which is 2). The TEMP value is given to LAG's second case. Thus, the second value for LAG is now equal to the first value of X. Next, SYSTAT moves the second value for X (which is 4) into TEMP.

Case 3. The TEMP value (4) goes into LAG, and the case 3 value of X (i.e., 6) goes into TEMP.

Case 4. The TEMP value (6) goes into LAG, and X's value (8) goes into TEMP.

The process continues until the last case is reached. The final X value goes into TEMP and is never used. The final LAG value is the penultimate X value.

10.21 Saving the last *n* cases of a file

This example shows you how to save the last ***n*** cases of an existing file to a new file. The program is useful if you regularly add data to a file and wish to do analyses on only the most recent cases.

The operation is done in two parts. The first establishes the total number of cases in the file (N). SYSTAT holds the end value of N from the first part in memory. It uses this value in the second part to determine which cases to save into the new file.

The program below saves the last 10 cases from USDATA into NEWFILE. Include the LIST REGION statement in the second part to show the cases that SYSTAT saves.

```
USE USDATA
HOLD
LET N=CASE
RUN

SAVE NEWFILE
IF N-CASE>=10 THEN DELETE
LIST REGION
RUN
```



```
                      REGION

 Case    41              4.000
 Case    42              4.000
 Case    43              4.000
 Case    44              4.000
 Case    45              4.000
 Case    46              4.000
 Case    47              4.000
 Case    48              4.000
 Case    49              4.000
 Case    50              4.000

   10 cases and   44 variables processed.
SYSTAT file created.
```

SYSTAT has saved the last ten cases for all the variables into NEWFILE.

10.22 Subgroup means

This program calculates the mean of the variable SPIRITS for each of the four regions in USDATA. On the last case for each group, we ask SYSTAT to calculate and print the mean, and reset SUM and N to 0. Of course, the same operation can be performed by using the STATISTICS command in **STATS**. In either case, the file must be sorted on the REGION variable when used with BY.

```
USE USDATA
BY REGION
HOLD
 LET N=N+1
 LET SUM=SUM+SPIRITS
 IF EOG THEN FOR
    LET MEAN=SUM/N
    PRINT "The mean spirits consumption rate"
    PRINT " for Region",REGION," is",MEAN
    LET SUM=0
    LET N=0
 NEXT
RUN
```



```
The mean spirits consumption rate
  for Region          1.000  is                  3.149
The mean spirits consumption rate
  for Region          2.000  is                  2.203
The mean spirits consumption rate
  for Region          3.000  is                  2.256
The mean spirits consumption rate
  for Region          4.000  is                  2.785

   50 cases and   46 variables processed.
No SYSTAT file created.
```

BY REGION sets REGION as the grouping variable for the IF EOG THEN FOR statements. After each case that is the last case in a REGION group (the last region 1 case, the last region 2 case, etc.), SYSTAT computes a mean from the sum it has computed for the group.

The BY command and the EOG variable are discussed in more detail in the previous chapter, **Subgroup processing**.

11 MACRO

MACRO 11

Overview

MACRO is a utility program for automating repetitive SYSTAT tasks, inserting SYSTAT output into letters, reports, or address labels, merging text files, generating SYSTAT submit files and creating SYSTAT system files. You can also program full screen data entry environments in **MACRO**. By combining these features into one macro you can create a single "front-end" for your application that would, for example, read in data from a data entry screen, analyze the data and format the results.

MACRO is intended for applications much beyond the capabilities of **DATA**. Paging through the examples in this chapter should make this clear. However, **MACRO** and **DATA** have similar command syntax. For this reason, we often present a **DATA** example and compare it with a **MACRO** example. We assume that you have experience using **DATA** BASIC and are familiar with its operation.

Introduction

MACRO operates two different ways. First, it can be used in conjunction with other SYSTAT procedures to take input from the user, create command files, and submit the command files to other SYSTAT procedures. Second, it can be used alone to manipulate data. For example, it can create subsets of SYSTAT data files based on user-specified conditions.

In this section we give a simple tutorial demonstrating the uses of **MACRO**. We recommend that you "get your feet wet" and try this tutorial right away. Even if you don't fully understand it now, it will give you an idea of the kinds of things that you can do with **MACRO**. After reading the other sections in this chapter, you might want to try it again.

The SYSTAT text editor **FEDIT** is useful for writing **MACRO** programs. Usually, you will create a command file in **FEDIT** and then submit it to **MACRO**. In this tutorial, you will learn the basic procedure for creating and editing command files with **FEDIT**. See the **FEDIT text editor** chapter in the *Getting Started* volume for more information.

11.1 Creating and submitting a command file

In this example, we write a macro that creates a command file and then submits it to **STATS**. This example also demonstrates **MACRO** text substitution.

Note that most of the lines in this macro are numbered. The numbers are optional, but we recommend that you use them. They are necessary if you use the %GOTO command. General SYSTAT commands such as USE, SAVE, etc. cannot be numbered. Also note that **MACRO** BASIC commands begin with a % sign while commands for other SYSTAT procedures do not. Pay careful attention to the use of % in this example.

Let's begin. If you have not already done so, enter **MACRO** by typing

```
MACRO
```

at the DOS prompt. Then type the following to invoke **FEDIT**:

```
FEDIT STATS.CMD
```

You should see a blank screen with the cursor at the top left corner and a menu bar across the bottom explaining what the different function keys do. You can use the arrow keys to move around the screen, and use the function and arrow keys in combination to block, move, copy, or delete text.

Now type the following macro:

```
10 %CLEAR
20 %PROMPT 'Enter name of file to process' AT 1 1
30 %INPUT FILE$ AT 1 40
40 %PROMPT 'Enter name of variable to process' AT 3 1
50 %INPUT VAR$ AT 3 40
60 %OUTPUT 'MEANS.CMD'
70 USE &FILE$
80 SAVE MEANS
90 STATS &VAR$
100 QUIT
110 %OUTPUT *
120 %SWITCHTO STATS 'MEANS.CMD'
RUN
```

When you finish, hit the F10 key to exit **FEDIT**. The menu bar is replaced by the message

```
Save changes? (Y/N)
```

Type

```
Y
```

You will see the message

```
File name? (return for current file)
```

Press Enter to save the file. You are now back in **MACRO**.

To execute the macro, type the following:

```
SUBMIT STATS
```

Line 10 clears the screen, and line 20 prompts you to enter a file name:

```
Enter the name of file to process
```

Type

```
US
```

and hit Enter. The %INPUT command (line 30) accepts the value US and places it in the variable FILE$. Now, line 40 prompts you to enter a variable name:

```
Enter name of variable to process
```

Type

```
RAIN
```

and hit Enter. The %INPUT command (line 50) stores RAIN in the variable VAR$.

Lines 60–110 use the FILE$ and VAR$ values you entered to create a command file MEANS.CMD which is echoed to the screen:

```
USE US
SAVE MEANS
STATS RAIN
QUIT
```


Line 120 switches you to the **STATS** procedure. SYSTAT executes the command file MEANS.CMD; the statistics for the variable RAIN are computed and appear on the screen along with the message:

```
Statistics have been saved
```

You are then returned to **MACRO**.

Text lines

The %OUTPUT command in line 60 tells **MACRO** to create a command file, MEANS.CMD, containing all subsequent **MACRO** *text lines* until it hits a second %OUTPUT command.

A **MACRO** text line is a numbered line that does not contain a % command. When **MACRO** encounters a text line, it prints the line to the current output device. Lines 70-100 in our example are **MACRO** text lines.

Text substitution

Lines 70 and 90 make use of *text substitution*, one of **MACRO**'s most powerful capabilities. When you prefix a variable name with an ampersand (&) in a **MACRO** text line, the value of that variable is substituted for the variable name in the output. In our example, line 70 says

```
USE &FILE$
```

We entered the value, so US is substituted for FILE$, and the following line is written to the command file:

```
USE US
```

Similarly, the value RAIN is substituted for VAR$ in line 90, so the command file contains the line:

```
STATS RAIN
```

See the "Text" section of this chapter for more information about text lines and text substitution.

11.2 Manipulating data

This example works entirely within **MACRO** and illustrates **MACRO**'s ability to read and write individual cases (rows) of a SYSTAT data file. We will save a subset of the USDATA datafile containing only the data for the Northeast region (REGION= 1) of the United States. Enter **FEDIT**:

```
FEDIT SUBSET.CMD
```

Now type the macro:

```
USE USDATA
SAVE REGION1
10 %READ
20 %IF REGION=1 THEN %WRITE
30 %IF EOF THEN %GOTO 50
40 %ELSE %GOTO 10
50 %PRINT 'Processing finished.'
60 %STOP
RUN
```

Use the F10 key as before to save the file and exit **FEDIT**. Now submit the macro:

```
SUBMIT SUBSET
```

The macro runs quickly and line 50 displays the following message:

```
Processing finished
```

Let's check to see whether the macro really worked. Type the following to enter **EDIT**:

```
SWITCHTO EDIT
```

If you then use the file REGION1,

```
USE REGION1
```

you will see that 9 cases, all with REGION=1, were saved into the file.

Let's go through the program line by line. The first two lines and the last line do not have line numbers. They are general SYSTAT commands, not **MACRO** BASIC commands, and must not be numbered. These three lines work as they would in **DATA**. See the "**MACRO** commands and functions" section of this chapter for more information.

Each time line 10 is executed, **MACRO** reads a single case from the data file, starting with the first case. Line 20 checks to see whether that case has the value 1 for the variable REGION. If so, the case is written to the SAVE file REGION1.SYS. Note that %READ and %WRITE work on whole cases rather than individual variables within cases. Pascal programmers should note that these commands are similar to the READLN and WRITELN statements.

Line 30 checks to see whether the end of the file (EOF) has been reached. If EOF is false, i.e., if the end of the file has not been reached, line 40 is executed. Line 40 passes control back to line 10, another case is read, and the process is repeated. Eventually the end of the file is reached (EOF is true), control goes to line 50, and **MACRO** indicates that "Processing is finished." Line 60 then tells **MACRO** to stop execution.

This macro illustrates **MACRO**'s ability to work with individual cases. This is one of the primary distinctions between **MACRO** and **DATA**. See the "File handling" section for more information.

Commands and functions

In this section we give a list of commands available in **MACRO.** These commands are divided into two categories: command level commands and **MACRO** BASIC commands. *Command level commands* are not BASIC commands and *cannot* be used with line numbers. *MACRO BASIC commands* all have the % prefix. Many of them are similar to **DATA** BASIC commands. These commands are discussed in detail in the **Appendix II,** the **MACRO command reference** and throughout this chapter.

We also give a list of the functions available in **MACRO.** Many of these functions have counterparts in **DATA.**

Command level commands

Both **DATA** and **MACRO** have commands that are not BASIC commands (they cannot be used with program line numbers) which can nonetheless be used in BASIC programs. In **MACRO** these are called "Command Level"commands. Here is a list of command level commands that work the same in both **MACRO** and **DATA:**

Command	*Action*
BY	Process by subgroups
DOS	Execute DOS command
DROP	Do not save named variables
ERASE	Erase lines of **MACRO** BASIC program
FORMAT	Set number of decimal places in output
HELP	Obtain online help
NEW	Clear workspace and close SYSTAT files
OUTPUT	Direct output to screen, printer, or file
QUIT	Exit **MACRO**
RUN	Execute **MACRO** without clearing the workspace
SAVE	Write data to a SYSTAT file
SUBMIT	Read and process command file
SWITCHTO	Change to another SYSTAT procedure and submit a command file
USE	Open SYSTAT file for input

MACRO has several command level commands not found in **DATA**:

`LIST`	List lines of the **MACRO** BASIC program
`LOAD`	Retrieve a **MACRO** program
`STORE`	Save a **MACRO** program

MACRO BASIC Commands

In contrast to command level commands, there are **MACRO** BASIC commands. These all have the % prefix, and many are similar to **DATA** BASIC commands. Here is a list of **MACRO** BASIC commands that have similar implementations in **DATA**:

`%DIM`	Declare a subscripted variable
`%ELSE`	Execute alternative when %IF condition is false
`%FOR`	Start a %FOR...%NEXT loop
`%GOTO`	Transfer program control to a specified line number
`%IF`	Execute %THEN statement if expression is true
`%LET`	Assign a value to a variable
`%NEXT`	Signal the end of a %FOR...%NEXT loop
`%PRINT`	Print variables and/or string expressions
`%STOP`	Halt the **MACRO** program

There are additional statements with no equivalents in **DATA** BASIC

`%CALL`	Transfer program control to a subroutine
`%CLEAR`	Clear the screen
`%DOS`	Execute a DOS command from within a macro
`%ENDSUB`	Declare the end of a subroutine
`%INPUT`	Read a value from the keyboard
`%INSERT`	Send text to the output device
`%LOAD`	Retrieve and execute a macro
`%MENU`	Present the user with a menu
`%PRINTNOLF`	Print without a line feed
`%PROMPT`	Print to a specified location on the screen
`%READ`	Read an observation from a SYSTAT file
`%OUTPUT:`	Direct output to screen, printer, or file
`%SUB`	Declare the start of a subroutine
`%SWITCHTO`	Change to another SYSTAT procedure
`%WRITE`	Write an observation to a SYSTAT file

Functions and operators

MACRO provides functions like those in **DATA**:

%ABS	Absolute value
%ACS	Arccosine
%ASN	Arcsine
%ATH	Arc hyperbolic tangent
%ATN	Arc tangent
%COS	Cosine
%EXP	Exponential function
%INT	Integer truncation
%LOG	Natural logarithm
%SIN	Sine
%SQR	Square root
%TAN	Tangent
%ZCF	Normal CDF
%ZIF	Inverse normal CDF
%ZRN	Returns a normal random variable

The following are multivariable functions. They work across cases (e.g., %AVG averages the values of several variables for the *same* case).

%AVG	Mean of non-missing variables
%MAX	Maximum value of the variables
%MIN	Minimum value of the variables
%MIS	Number of missing values for variables
%STD	Standard deviation of non-missing variables
%SUM	Sum of non-missing variables

There are five character functions in **MACRO** not found in **DATA**. They are valid only when used with the %LET command. These functions are discussed in detail in the "String manipulation" section of this chapter:

%CHR	Return specified ASCII character
%EDIT	Reverse value type (character <—> numeric)
%INDEX	Return the position of a string in a character variable
%SUBSTR	Return a portion of a character variable
WITH	Concatenate strings

There are boolean (true/false) variables that also appear in **DATA:**

BOG	True if beginning of a BY group, otherwise false
EOG	True if end of a BY group, otherwise false
BOF	True if beginning of the USE file, otherwise false
EOF	True if end of a USE file, otherwise false

Note that there are many **DATA** features with no **MACRO** counterparts:

APPEND	HOLD	RANK
ARRAY	INPUT	REPEAT
CASE	LABEL	RSEED
CODE	LRECL	SORT
DELETE	NOTE	STANDARDIZE
DIAGONAL	PUT	TRANSPOSE
		TYPE

Text Substitution

MACRO text substitution allows you to print the value of a variable within a string. Here is an example which does *not* use text substitution. We give both the **DATA** and **MACRO** programs.

DATA

```
REPEAT 1
LET NAME$ = 'Jack'
PRINT 'NAME$ and Jill'
RUN
```

MACRO

```
%LET NAME$ = 'Jack'
%PRINT 'NAME$ and Jill'
RUN
```

Note that NAME$ ends in a dollar sign because it is a character variable. The output from both examples is:

```
NAME$ and Jill
```

Suppose you want to print the *value* of NAME$ rather than the word "NAME$." **DATA** can only do this if you want the value at the end of the PRINT statement. **MACRO**, however, offers text substitution. Simply prefix the variable name with an ampersand (&):

```
%LET NAME$ = 'Jack'
%PRINT '&NAME$ and Jill'
RUN
```

The output is:

```
Jack and Jill
```

The ampersand (&) prefixed to NAME$ tells **MACRO** that NAME$ is a variable rather than a word of text. **MACRO** prints the value of that variable instead of the variable name. Any **MACRO** string expression can use text substitution. The ampersand can be used only in conjunction with text substitution. If a variable does not follow the &, then the character is ignored. Text substitution works with numeric as well as character variables.

Here are a few more examples. The commands:

```
%LET NUM = value
%PRINT 'expression'
```

produce the following output with the given values and expressions:

Value	*Expression*	*Output*
10	'Num is &NUM'	Num is 10.000
10	'Num is &'	Num is
10	'Num is & NUM'	Num is NUM
10	'Num is NUM'	Num is NUM

Text substitution is also available in text lines (discussed below).

Text lines

There are two kinds of statements in **MACRO**. The first is any legal **MACRO** BASIC statement like %IF, %FOR, etc. The second is a **MACRO** text line. While a **MACRO** BASIC statement must be executed, a **MACRO** text line is simply printed to the current output device. Text lines are helpful when making submit files, front ends for SYSTAT users, and a variety of other tasks.

A **MACRO** text line appears on a numbered line, does not begin with a "%" command, and contains any combination of text and variables. When **MACRO** encounters a numbered line that doesn't start with a %, it recognizes the line as a text line and prints it to the current output device (i.e. the screen, printer or file).

You may use text substitution (discussed above) in text lines. However, you *cannot* use text substitution with subscripted variables.

MACRO text lines can be placed anywhere in a macro. This means that a macro can have several text lines, then several lines of commands, then more text. The text lines are routed to the output device (i.e. the screen, printer, or file).

Undefined variables

If a variable in a text line is undefined, **MACRO** changes the variable name to a null, interpreting the text as if the variable name did not exist. For example, the variable VAR in the following program is undefined:

```
10 %FOR X = 1 to 2
20  PRINT &VAR
30 %NEXT
RUN
```

Therefore, SYSTAT treats it as a null and responds:

```
PRINT
PRINT
```

Uninitialized variables

Notice that an *undefined* variable works differently than an *uninitialized* variable. Variables are defined when they are used in any **MACRO** BASIC line (that is, in any line with a %). A variable is initialized to missing when defined.

Here, the variable VAR is defined since it appears in line 40. However, VAR is not initialized until after the text line PRINT &VAR. Thus, a missing value (i.e., a period) is printed.

```
10 %FOR X = 1 to 2
20  PRINT &VAR
30 %NEXT
40 %LET VAR = 1
RUN
```

The output is:

```
PRINT .
PRINT .
```

11.3 Using text substitution in text lines

For a simple example, enter the following statements:

```
10 %LET PVAL = 0.044
20 %LET ANALYSIS$ = 'ANOVA'
30 The results of your &ANALYSIS$
40 are at the &PVAL probability level.
RUN
```

Looks kind of strange, doesn't it? After typing RUN the following message appears on the screen:

```
The results of your ANOVA
are at the 0.044 probability level.
```

Inserting text from ASCII files: %INSERT

The %INSERT command allows you to print text from ASCII files in your **MACRO** program output. If you have extended text that you want printed when you run a macro, but do not want to include the text in the macro itself, place the text in an ASCII file and %INSERT this file from within your macro. The syntax of the %INSERT command is:

```
[line #] %INSERT filename,
   / START='string1', END='string2'
```

If you include path information in your filename, you must enclose it in single or double quotation marks. Some examples are:

```
%INSERT LETTER
%INSERT '\SYSTAT\LETTER.DAT'
```

11.4 Using text substitution with an insert file

This example is similar to 11.3 but uses the following insert file, TEXTFILE.DAT:

```
The results of your &ANALYSIS
are at the &PVAL probability level.
```

The **MACRO** commands are:

```
10 %LET PVAL = 0.044
20 %LET ANALYSIS$ = 'ANOVA'
30 %INSERT TEXTFILE
RUN
```

The output produced is:

```
The results of your ANOVA
are at the 0.044 probability level.
```

If you only want to print part of a text file, use the START and END options. With the following commands, all text starting with the first occurrence of the letter A and ending with the first occurrence of the letter B is printed to the output device:

```
%INSERT 'MY.TXT' / START='A', END='B'
```

If you include text lines in your **MACRO** program, you *must* have line numbers! You can skip the line numbers if you use %INSERT files instead of text lines.

11.5 Creating a text file

The following program prompts you for information and stores that information in a text file.

Program command	*What MACRO does*
`10 %OUTPUT 'TEST.DAT'`	Sends all following output to the file TEST.DAT
`20 Tests to do:`	Prints "Tests to do:" to the output file.
`30`	Prints a blank line to the output file.
`40 %PROMPT 'ENTER TEST:'`	Prints "ENTER TEST: " to the screen and waits for a user to enter a word.
`50 %INPUT TEST$`	Stores the word into the variable TEST$.
`60 &TEST$`	Prints the contents of the variable TEST to the output file.
`70 %IF TEST$<>' ' THEN, %GOTO 40`	If the user entered a word (more than just a carriage return) then goes to line 40.
`80`	Prints a blank line to the output file.
`90 Do those tests.`	Prints the line "Do those tests." to the output file.
`100 %OUTPUT *`	Closes the output file and redirectsoutput to the screen.
`RUN`	Executes macro.

SYSTAT responds:

```
Tests to do:

Enter test:
```

SYSTAT echoes all text lines (20, 30, 60, 80, and 90) to the screen as it writes them to TEST.DAT. Enter three tests, ANOVA, MANOVA, and TTEST, followed by a blank line to terminate input. The screen should read:

```
Tests to do:

Enter test:
ANOVA
ANOVA
Enter test:
MANOVA
MANOVA
Enter test:
TTEST
TTEST
Enter test:


Do those tests
```

The text file TEST.DAT in which we saved the information contains:

```
Tests to do:

ANOVA
MANOVA
TTEST

Do those tests
```

MACRO's screen handling capabilities allow you to write interactive programs. The commands discussed in this section allow you to clear the screen, print to the screen, prompt the user for information, present the user with a menu, and read input entered from the keyboard.

Clearing the screen

The %CLEAR command clears the screen and moves the cursor to the 1st row and first column. Its syntax is:

```
[line#] CLEAR
```

Presenting the user with a menu

The %MENU command writes a menu to the screen. A menu allows the user to choose one of several items. Its syntax is

```
[line#] %MENU var 'menu title',
      / 'choice1','choice2'...'choicen'
```

where *menu title* is the title of the menu, *choice1* thru *choicen* are the menu items, and *var* is the numeric variable that holds the menu choice. For example, suppose your macro contains the line

```
%MENU CHOICE, 'Choose a test',
      / 'ANOVA','MANOVA','TTEST'
```

When this line is executed the following appears on the screen:

```
Choose a test

1 ANOVA
2 MANOVA
3 TTEST
```

The user cursors to the choice she wants and presses Enter. The appropriate value (1, 2, or 3) is saved in the variable CHOICE. See Example 11.26 for an advanced application of %MENU.

Printing variables and strings

The %PRINT command prints variables and text strings. Its syntax is:

```
[line#] %PRINT [var | 'string']
```

Examples are:

```
%PRINT
%PRINT AGE SEX
```

The first example prints a blank. The second example prints the values of the variables AGE and SEX.

You can use text substitution with %PRINT. Here are some sample commands and output:

```
%LET NAME$='JED'
%PRINT '&NAME$ went to buy a loaf of bread'
```

```
Jed went to buy a loaf of bread
```

The %PRINTNOLF command prints variables or strings without adding a carriage return or line feed at the end of the line. It has the same syntax as PRINT.

Prompting the user

The %PROMPT command sends a string or variable value to the screen. Its syntax is:

```
[line#] %PROMPT 'string' | var [AT row,col, INVERSE]
```

Row and *col* move the cursor to a specified row and column on the screen before writing. The first row and first column are at the top left of the screen. Valid coordinates are 1 thru 25 for rows and 1 thru 80 for columns. You may use numbers or numeric variables to specify row and column coordinates. The INVERSE option provides reverse high-lighting. Examples are:

```
%PROMPT 'This is the order entry form'
%PROMPT LASTNAME$ AT 5 1
%PROMPT TOTAL AT 10 10 INVERSE

%LET NAME$ ='John'
%PROMPT 'Is your name &NAME$?'
```

You can use numeric or character variables in the string expression. If you want the prompt to contain the value of a variable, you must use the & symbol with the variable name, as in the last example.

Inputting data from the keyboard

The %INPUT command reads the value of a variable entered from the keyboard. It usually follows a %PROMPT command. Its syntax is

```
[line#] %INPUT var [AT row col]
```

The value is read from the screen and stored in the variable *var*. *Row* and *col* move the cursor to a specified position before reading the value. The first row and first column are at the top left of the screen. Valid coordinates are 1 thru 25 for rows and 1 thru 80 for columns. Here are some examples:

```
%INPUT AGE
%INPUT AGE AT 5 10
%INPUT AGE AT VARX,VARY
```

The second %INPUT command above places the cursor at the location 5, 10 and waits for the user to input a value for AGE. The last %INPUT command uses numeric variables to specify screen location. You may *not* use subscripted variables. Nor may you specify the screen location with a combination of numbers and variables. For example, VAR1+12, VAR2+3 is not a valid screen location.

11.6 Prompting the user for a filename.

The example below shows a short macro that clears the screen, prompts the user for the name of a SYSTAT file to process, and then prints the name of that file to the screen.

```
10 %CLEAR
20 %PROMPT 'Enter SYSTAT file name:' AT 2 1
30 %INPUT FNAME$ AT 2 30
40 %PROMPT '&FNAME$ will be processed.' AT 3 1
RUN
```

Here is the output (SYSNAME is entered by the user):

```
Enter SYSTAT file name: SYSNAME
SYSNAME will be processed.
```

11.7 Creating a batch file

Let's move ahead to a more complicated example. Suppose you want to create a batch file named ANOVA.CMD that executes a one-way analysis of variance. You want to be prompted by a macro for all of the information needed to run the ANOVA, and you want the macro to write that information to the batch file.

```
FORMAT = 0
10 %CLEAR
20 %PROMPT 'Enter SYSTAT file name: ' AT 1 1
30 %INPUT FILENAME$ AT 1 31
40 %PROMPT 'Enter the DV: ' AT 2 1
50 %INPUT DV$ AT 2 31
60 %PROMPT 'Enter the IV: ' AT 3 1
70 %INPUT IV$ AT 3 31
100 %PROMPT 'Enter command file name: ' AT 5 1
110 %INPUT COMMAND$ AT 5 31
120 %OUTPUT '&COMMAND$'
130 USE &FILENAME$
140 CATEGORY &IV$
150 MODEL &DV$ = CONSTANT + &IV$
160 NOTE 'HERE ARE YOUR RESULTS...'
170 ESTIMATE
180 %OUTPUT *
RUN
```

Here are the results, the words in boldface are entered by the user:

```
Enter SYSTAT file name:    USSTATS
Enter the DV:              SPIRITS
Enter the IV:              REGION
Enter command file name:   ANOVA.CMD
```

The following lines are written to the batch file:

```
USE USSTATS
CATEGORY REGION
MODEL SPIRITS = CONSTANT + REGION
NOTE 'HERE ARE YOUR RESULTS...'
ESTIMATE
```

Reading and writing SYSTAT files

With a **DATA** BASIC program, the entire set of commands is applied to each case in the data file. With **MACRO**, however, you specify when to read a case from the USE file and when to write a case to the SAVE file. This offers a great degree of flexibility.

The %READ command reads one record of data from a SYSTAT data file. Its syntax is

```
[line#] %READ
```

The %READ command reads an entire case at a time—you cannot select variables.

The %WRITE command writes an entire case to the file that is specified with the SAVE command. Its syntax is:

```
[line#] %WRITE
```

Notice that the WRITE command does not have any parameters. You may not specify which variables to WRITE to the file. WRITE writes *all* variables that appear in your macro to the SYSTAT file. You can DROP variables, however, if you want only a subset of them to appear in your final SYSTAT file (remember, after you DROP a variable, you cannot make any reference to it).

SAVE files are closed when processing is finished. You may USE a SAVE file after you type RUN.

11.8 Transforming a variable

Here are two programs that perform the same task. The program on the left is a **DATA** program while the program on the right is a **MACRO** program. In this example, the file A.SYS has the variable X:

DATA

```
USE A
SAVE B
LET NEWX = X^2
RUN
```

MACRO

```
USE A
SAVE B
10 %READ
20 %LET NEWX = X^2
30 %WRITE
40 %IF EOF THEN %GOTO 60
50 %GOTO 10
60 %STOP
RUN
```

Both programs create a new variable NEWX which is the square of X.

11.9 Generating random numbers

Here is another example of reading from and writing to a SYSTAT file. Both programs store five random numbers in the variable A in a file called RANDOM.SYS:

DATA

```
SAVE RANDOM
REPEAT 5
LET A = ZRN
RUN
```

MACRO

```
SAVE RANDOM
%FOR I = 1 TO 5
%LET A = %ZRN
%WRITE
%NEXT
RUN
```

11.10 Using a FOR...NEXT loop to work across cases

Suppose the file AFILE.SYS has the following data:

CASE	*A*
1	5
2	20
3	30
4	40
5	50

The following two programs perform the same operation:

DATA

```
USE AFILE
IF A = 5 THEN PRINT,
'A = 5'
ELSE PRINT 'A <> 5'
RUN
```

MACRO

```
USE AFILE
%FOR I = 1 to 5
%READ
%IF A = 5 THEN %PRINT,
'A = 5'
%ELSE %PRINT 'A <> 5'
%NEXT
RUN
```

The output from both programs is:

```
A = 5
A <> 5
A <> 5
A <> 5
A <> 5
```

This example shows how the %FOR...%NEXT loop in **MACRO** can work across cases (this is not available in **DATA**).

Creating, saving, and using MACRO command files

MACRO reads two types of command files. First, you can SUBMIT a text file of commands just as you would in any other SYSTAT procedure. These command files are in ASCII format and are simply a list of SYSTAT commands. Each time the command file is submitted, SYSTAT must interpret each command before execution.

Alternatively, you can store macro commands in a file which has a special binary format. We say that such files are ***tokenized.*** Tokenized files are processed much more rapidly than ASCII files. Use tokenized files for large macros that you will use frequently and that you won't have to modify often. Tokenized files have the .TOK extension and are created with the STORE command:

```
STORE filename / NOCODE
```

NOCODE is optional and saves a binary copy of a macro without storing the source text with it. SYSTAT processes such files more quickly, but they cannot be listed.

The LOAD command is used to submit a tokenized file:

```
LOAD filename
```

If your filename includes path information, you must enclose it in quotes. LOAD clears all **MACRO** commands in memory prior to loading the macro.

11.11 Loading and running a tokenized macro

Suppose the file COMMANDS.CMD has the following commands:

```
%FOR I = 1 TO 50
   %READ
   %WRITE
%NEXT
```

This list of commands can be stored in the special **MACRO** file format with the following commands:

```
SUBMIT COMMANDS
STORE AMACRO
```

SYSTAT reads all commands from COMMANDS.CMD into the file AMACRO.TOK. COMMANDS.CMD and AMACRO.TOK contain identical information—only the file format is different. To execute the macro, type:

```
USE MEDICAL
SAVE NEWFILE
LOAD AMACRO
RUN
```

MACRO can perform several types of string manipulation, including appending strings, selecting subsets of characters from strings, converting numbers to strings, and converting strings to numbers.

Returning a specified ASCII character

The %CHR function returns the ASCII character corresponding to the number you choose. The number can be between 1 and 255. This function can be used only with the %LET command. Its syntax is:

```
%LET var = %CHR (expression)
```

Variables and/or numbers may be used as the expression. Examples are:

```
%LET A$ = %CHR(67)
%LET B$ = %CHR(I+40)
```

Locating a string in a character variable

The %INDEX returns a number identifying the location of a specified string in a character variable. It is valid only with the %LET command. Its syntax is:

```
%LET var = %INDEX(var$,'string')
```

Var$ is a character variable, *string* is the string you wish to locate in that variable, and *var* is the numeric variable that stores the string location.

Here is an example:

```
%LET A$='ABCXD'
%LET LOCATION=%INDEX(A$,'BC')
```

In this example LOCATION gets the value 2 because the string BC begins with the second character of ABCXD. Here is another example:

```
%LET A$='ABCXD'
%LET LOCATION=%INDEX(A$,'rrr')
```

Here, LOCATION is missing (i.e., it gets the value .) because the string rrr does not appear in ABCXD.

Returning a portion of a character variable

The %SUBSTR command is used with the %LET command to assign a subset of characters from one character variable to another character variable. Its syntax is:

```
%LET var1$ = %SUBSTR(var2$,location,numchar)
```

Var2$ is the character variable that the substring is taken from, *location* is the starting location of the substring, and *numchar* is the number of characters that will be assigned to *var1$*, beginning at the starting location.

Here is an example:

```
LET X$='ABC'
LET A$=%SUBSTR(X$,2,1)
```

The %SUBSTR command tells **MACRO** to begin at the second character of the string ABC (i.e., B) and to read 1 character. Thus, the value 'B' is assigned to A$. Let's look at another example:

```
LET X$='STRING'
LET A$=%SUBSTR(X$,3,2)
```

This time **MACRO** starts from the third character (i.e., R) and reads 2 characters. Thus, the value 'RI' is assigned to A$.

%SUBSTR can access only the first twelve characters of a string. Statements like the following are not valid:

```
LET X$='ABCDEFGHIJKLMNOPQ'
LET A$=%SUBSTR(X$,15,1)
```

and

```
LET X$='ABCDEFGHIJKLMNOPQ'
LET A$=%SUBSTR(X$,5,10)
```

The first example fails, because it tries to access the fifteenth character. The second example won't work, because starting at the fifth character and reading 10 characters takes **MACRO** beyond the 12 character limit.

Example 11.13 demonstrates the %SUBSTRING command.

Concatenating strings

The WITH command is used to join two or more strings. It can only be used with the %LET command. Its syntax is:

```
%LET var1$=var2$ WITH var3$…WITH varn$
```

For example suppose we have variables with the following values

Variable	*Value*
A$	'A'
B$	'B'
C$	'C'
WORD$	'WORD'

then the following command assigns ABC to D$:

```
%LET D$ = A$ WITH B$ WITH C$
```

The next command assigns the value A WORD to D$ (%CHR(32) returns a blank)

```
%LET D$ = A$ WITH %CHR(32) WITH WORD$
```

Special formats

The %EDIT command supports a variety of special formats. It changes the format of an existing variable and stores the newly formatted values in a new variable. For example, if you have a variable containing six-digit codes such as 011375, you can use %EDIT convert these codes to character values representing dates, i.e., 01/13/75. The syntax of %EDIT is:

```
%LET destvar = %EDIT(sourcevar,format)
```

Sourcevar is the original variable, *destvar* is the newly formatted variable, *format* is the format you want the the new variable to have.

You can choose from the following formats:

Format	*Source vartype*	*Destination vartype*	*Inserted characters*
DOLLAR	numeric	character	$,
COMMA	numeric	character	,
YYDDD	numeric	character	.
MMDDYY	numeric	character	/
POUND	numeric	character	£,
YEN	numeric	character	Y,
SSN	numeric	character	-
#fw.nd	numeric	character	,
NUMBER	character	numeric	none

DOLLAR converts numeric variables to character variables representing dollar amounts (e.g., 45678.23 is converted to $45,678.23). POUND and YEN work similarly . COMMA converts numbers to character values with commas inserted (e.g., 23400 is converted to 23,400). NUMBER converts character values with numeric characters to numeric values (see below for more information).SSN converts numbers to character values representing Social Security numbers (e.g., 123456789 is converted to 123–45–6789). MMDDYY translates numeric variables into dates. YYDDD translates numeric variables into year and day format (e.g., 90213 is converted to 90.213—the 213th of 1990). The numeric format (*#fw.nd*) translates numbers to characters and allows you to specify the field width and the decimal accuracy of the variables you are translating. The default decimal point accuracy is three places. You can specify any accuracy from 1 to 11 as long as the total width of the number being translated does not exceed 12 characters.

Here are some examples. Suppose that you issue the following command:

```
%LET X$ = expression
```

The following table shows what X$ equals with the given *expression*:

Expression	*Value*	*X$*
%EDIT(VALUE,DOLLAR)	12345.67890	$12,345.679
%EDIT(VALUE,DOLLAR#12.0)	12345.67890	$12,345
%EDIT(VALUE,COMMA)	12345.67890	12,345.679
%EDIT(VALUE,POUND)	12345.67890	£12,345.679
%EDIT(VALUE,YEN)	12345.67890	Y12,345.679
%EDIT(VALUE,#12.5)	12345.67890	12,345.67890
%EDIT(VALUE,SSN)	123456789	123-45-6789
%EDIT(VALUE,MMDDYY)	023187	02/31/87
%EDIT(VALUE,YYDDD)	87345	87.345
%EDIT(VALUE$,NUMBER)	'123123'	123123.000

The NUMBER format

The NUMBER format converts character values to numeric values. It can only convert characters that are numbers. Illegal characters in a character-to-number translation are ignored. If the first character is illegal, the numeric variable is set to missing. Otherwise, the numeric variable is the value representing all characters up to the first "illegal" value. Here are some examples:

Commands	*Results*
%LET X$ = '$123123.0'	
%LET X = %EDIT(X$,NUMBER)	X = .
%LET X$ = '123,123.0'	
%LET X = %EDIT(X$,NUMBER)	X = 123.000
%LET X$ = '12/12/83'	
%LET X = %EDIT(X$,NUMBER)	X = 12.000

In the first example, the first character ($) is illegal (it is not a number), so X is set to missing. In the second example, the comma (the 4th character) is illegal, so only the first three characters are used, and X gets the value 123. In the third example, the slash is illegal, so only the 1 and 2 are read, and X gets the value 12.

Subroutines

MACRO allows you to direct program control to a named *subroutine*. A subroutine is a block of **MACRO** code that usually performs a single operation and is thus a logical unit of program organization. Subroutines are one of the most basic elements of a good structured programming style. They make large, complex programs modular and therefore easier to read, understand, and modify. Even smaller programs benefit from subroutines.

Control is passed to a subroutine when it is called from the main program. This is similar to the GOTO command which passes control to another numbered line of the program.

The subroutine block must have a name, begin with the %SUB command, and end with the %ENDSUB command. The %SUB has the following syntax:

```
[line#] %SUB name
```

Name is the subroutine names.

The %ENDSUB command has the following syntax:

```
[line#] %ENDSUB
```

The %CALL command transfers control to a subroutine. It appears in the main macro program and has the following syntax:

```
[line#] %CALL name
```

Name is the name of the subroutine that is being called.

The line numbers (if you use them) for a subroutine must fall between the numbers of that subroutine's %SUB and %ENDSUB commands. For example, the following subroutine will not work:

```
100 %SUB PROBLEM
110 %LET I = I + 1
120 %LET J = J + 1
130 %LET K = K + 1
140 %PRINT 'J = &J'
190 %PRINT 'K = &K'
160 %PRINT 'L = &L'
170 %ENDSUB
```

Line 190 is not considered part of the subroutine. If you have a subroutine that is acting strangely, double check your line numbers.

11.12 Subroutines vs. GOTO

The following two programs do the same thing. They both prompt the user to enter a 1, 2, or 3; 1 switches control to **STATS**, 2 switches control to **MGLH**, and 3 stops execution of the macro. The first program uses GOTO statements:

```
 10 %PRINT 'Enter 1 to go to STATS'
 20 %PRINT 'Enter 2 to go to MGLH'
 30 %PRINT 'Enter 3 to QUIT'
 40 %INPUT CHOICE
 50 %IF CHOICE = 1 THEN %GOTO 100
 60 %ELSE %IF CHOICE = 2 THEN %GOTO 120
 70 %ELSE %IF CHOICE = 3 THEN %GOTO 90
 80 %GOTO 10
 90 %STOP
100 %SWITCHTO STATS
110 %GOTO 10
120 %SWITCHTO MGLH
130 %GOTO 10
```

The following program uses subroutines (lines 100–120 and 130–50).

```
 10 %PRINT 'Enter 1 to go to STATS'
 20 %PRINT 'Enter 2 to go to MGLH'
 30 %PRINT 'Enter 3 to QUIT'
 40 %INPUT CHOICE
 50 %IF CHOICE = 1 THEN %CALL XFERSTAT
 60 %IF CHOICE = 2 THEN %CALL XFERMGLH
 70 %ELSE %IF CHOICE = 3 THEN %GOTO 90
 80 %GOTO 10
 90 %STOP
100 %SUB XFERSTAT
110 %SWITCHTO STATS
120 %ENDSUB
130 %SUB XFERMGLH
140 %SWITCHTO MGLH
150 %ENDSUB
```

So why use subroutines rather than GOTO statements? First, if you use GOTO statements, and you change line numbers in your program, you have to change all your GOTO statements as well. This is not necessary with subroutines. Second, you may want to execute the same code in many different places in a program. Subroutines allow you to execute a series of commands any number of times with only one copy of the code. Third, building a program with subroutines allows you to develop a macro with manageable blocks. Fourth, subroutines can be recursive. In other words, a subroutine can CALL itself. If you are familiar with recursive programming in a traditional programming language (i.e. Pascal or BASIC) see the note regarding recursive macros in the "Important operating tips" section of this chapter.

11.13 Finding the mean of a variable

Here we modify Example 11.1. Recall that 11.1 prompted the user for names of a datafile and a variable and then found the mean value for that variable. This time we write a subroutine, GETVAL, to get information from the user.

```
10 %SUB GETVAL
20 %CLEAR
30 %PROMPT 'Enter name of file to process' at 1 1
40 %INPUT FILE$ AT 1 40
50 %PROMPT 'Enter name of variable to process' at 3 1
60 %INPUT VAR$ AT 3 40
70 %ENDSUB
```

This subroutine is simply the input sequence from the original program, transformed to a subroutine by adding the %SUB and %ENDSUB commands.

We also add a subroutine, CHECKEM, to check for errors in user input:

```
80 %SUB CHECKEM
90 %CLEAR
100 %PRINT 'The file and variables you specified are:'
110 %PRINT 'FILE: &FILE$'
120 %PRINT 'VARIABLE: &VAR$'
130 %PROMPT 'Are these correct?' AT 5 1
140 %INPUT VALID$ AT 5 20
150 %ENDSUB
```

This subroutine prints the values of the last file and variable input and asks the user if they are correct.

The main body of the program then becomes:

```
160 %CLEAR
170 %CALL GETVAL
180 %CALL CHECKEM
190 %LET FIRST$=%SUBSTR(VALID$,1,1)
210 %IF FIRST$='n' OR FIRST$='N' THEN %GOTO 170
220 %OUTPUT 'MEANS.CMD'
230 USE &FILE$
240 SAVE MEANS
250 STATS &VAR$
260 QUIT
270 %OUTPUT *
280 %SWITCHTO STATS 'MEANS.CMD'
RUN
```

Line 170 calls the GETVAL subroutine. Line 180 calls CHECKEM . If the user indicates that the file and variable are correct, the program proceeds. If the file and variable are not correct the GETVAL subroutine is called again, and the user can enter another value.

This example also demonstrates the use of the %SUBSTR string manipulation function discussed in the previous section. Line 190 takes VALID$ and assigns its first character to a new variable named FIRST$. An English translation of this line is, "Find the variable name VALID$, go to the first position in the character string, and read one character. Then assign that character to the new variable FIRST$." This allows the macro to deal with either "y" or "yes" as input values. Note that in line 210 we are careful to check for both upper and lower case responses. Finally, you should notice that we declare the subroutines before the main body of the macro. This prevents error messages caused by an undefined variable.

Executing a macro from another SYSTAT procedure

The MACRO command

You can execute a macro from another SYSTAT procedure with the MACRO command. It has the following syntax:

```
MACRO commandfile / statement1, statement2,...
```

Commandfile is a file containing **MACRO** commands. The *statements* are optional additional **MACRO** statements to execute with your command file. You can specify up to 400 **MACRO** statements with the MACRO command.

You cannot use the MACRO command within **MACRO.**

When you issue a MACRO command, the command file you specify is sent to **MACRO** for processing. **MACRO** interprets all commands and submits all lines of text substitution to the procedure from which you invoked the macro. Macros submitted from procedures other than **MACRO** must have line numbers.

11.14 Automating repetitive tasks with a macro

If you have a sequence of commands that you often enter in SYSTAT, you can automate the sequence with a macro. Suppose you often analyze the distribution of a variable in **GRAPH** with a set of commands such as:

```
USE filename
SELECT variable = value
STEM variable
BOX variable
PPLOT variable
```

You can automate the process by calling the following macro, DISTRIB.CMD, from **GRAPH**:

```
100 USE &FILENAME$
110 SELECT &SELVAR$ = &SELVAL
120 STEM &VAR$
130 BOX &VAR$
140 PPLOT &VAR$
```

DISTRIB.CMD contains **MACRO** text lines and uses **MACRO**'s text substitution capability. As you will see, you assign the file name, variable names, and values when you call the **MACRO**.

The macro DISTRIB.CMD could be executed from **GRAPH** with this command:

```
MACRO DISTRIB / 60 %LET FILENAME$='US';
                  70 %LET VAR$ = 'RAIN';
                  80 %LET SELVAR$ = 'REGION$';
                  90 %LET SELVAL$ = "'NEW ENGLAND'"
```

The MACRO command invokes the processing of the commands in the file DISTRIB.CMD. The commands listed after the slash are inserted at the beginning of the macro and the macro becomes:

```
60 %LET FILENAME$ = 'US'
70 %LET VAR$ = 'RAIN'
80 %LET SELVAR$ = 'REGION$'
90 %LET SELVAL$ = "'NEW ENGLAND'"
100 USE &FILENAME$
110 SELECT &SELVAR$ = &SELVAL
120 STEM &VAR$
130 BOX &VAR$
140 PPLOT &VAR$
```

The following **GRAPH** commands are executed:

```
USE US
SELECT REGION$ = 'NEW ENGLAND'
STEM RAIN
BOX RAIN
PPLOT RAIN
```


11.15 Conditionally executing commands

Here is another example of a macro that conditionally executes commands in the **GRAPH**. First, here are the contents of DISTRIB.CMD:

```
100 USE &FILENAME$
110 STEM &VAR$
120 %IF EXTENDED = 1 THEN %FOR
130   BOX &VAR$
140   PPLOT &VAR$
150 %NEXT
```

Invoke DISTRIB.CMD in **GRAPH** with this command:

```
MACRO DISTRIB / %LET VAR$ = 'DOLLARS';
                   %LET FILENAME$ = 'SYSFILE.SYS';
                   %LET EXTENDED = 1
```

In this example, you invoke extended graphical analysis by assigning the EXTENDED variable a value of 1. If you do not desire extended analysis, then you can assign EXTENDED any other value.

11.16 A very short macro

Here is another example of a correct (and very short) macro command file (called MYMACRO.CMD):

```
5 USE &FILENAME$
```

You can invoke this file from **GRAPH** with the MACRO command:

```
MACRO MYMACRO / %LET FILENAME$ = 'SYSFILE';
                   10 %LET A$ = 'IV';
                   20 %LET B$ = 'DV';
                   30 PLOT &B$ * &A$
```

The commands listed after the slash are executed with the macro. You can execute the same set of commands if you put them in the file MYMACRO.CMD as follows:

```
 5 USE SYSFILE
10 %LET A$ = 'IV'
20 %LET B$ = 'DV'
30 PLOT &B$ * &A$
```

Then invoke MYMACRO.CMD (from **GRAPH**) with the command:

```
MACRO MYMACRO
```

Command priority

In order to use the MACRO command correctly, you must understand how SYSTAT processes it. First, the command file and all of the appended **MACRO** BASIC commands are sent to **MACRO** for processing. Second, **MACRO** interprets and integrates the command file with the appended **MACRO** BASIC commands. Third, **MACRO** executes all commands that are not text substitution. Fourth, all text substitution commands are sent to the "host"procedure (the procedure from which you invoke the macro) for execution. Here are the types of commands listed in order from highest priority (executed first) to lowest (executed last):

1) Command level commands from the MACRO command.
2) Command level commands from the macro file.
3) Unnumbered **MACRO** BASIC statements from the MACRO command.
4) Unnumbered **MACRO** BASIC statements from the macro file.
5) Numbered **MACRO** BASIC commands from the MACRO command are placed in the logical order among numbered statements in your macro file. You cannot override numbered statements in your macro file with commands from the MACRO command.

11.17 Integrating lines from a MACRO command into a macro

The following example demonstrates how SYSTAT integrates the lines from a macro file with the commands from the MACRO command. This example is *not* representative of a typical macro because there is no text substitution and, hence, no commands are sent to the "host" procedure. This example does show, however, how SYSTAT orders the commands for execution. These are the commands in the file MYMACRO.CMD:

```
%PROMPT 'Another unnumbered line'
20 %PROMPT 'Line 20'
30 %PROMPT 'Line 30'
40 %PROMPT '40 FROM CMDFILE'
```

Here is the command invoking MYMACRO:

```
MACRO MYMACRO / %PROMPT,
                    'An unnumbered line';
                    10 %PROMPT 'Line 10';
                    40 %PROMPT '40 FROM COMMAND'
```

Here are the commands executed:

```
%PROMPT 'An unnumbered line'
%PROMPT 'Another unnumbered line'
10 %PROMPT 'Line 10'
20 %PROMPT 'Line 20'
30 %PROMPT 'Line 30'
40 %PROMPT '40 FROM CMDFILE'
```

Executing a tokenized macro

So far we have discussed how to execute macros that are in ASCII format. You can also execute tokenized macros (macros you have saved with the STORE command) with the MACRO command. To do this, do not specify a command file with the MACRO command. Rather, enter a %LOAD command as your first optional command. For example,

```
MACRO / %LOAD 'TOKEN.TOK';
        %LET A$ = 'AGE'
```

In this example the commands from TOKEN.TOK are read into memory and integrated with the %LET A$ = 'AGE' command. Note that if the file TOKEN.CMD (in ASCII format) has the same commands as TOKEN.TOK, the following command will yield identical results:

```
MACRO 'TOKEN.CMD' / %LET A$ = 'AGE'
```

Important operating tips

Program length limitations

A single macro file can have a maximum length of 400 lines. You can, however, %LOAD a second macro, and then a third, ***ad infinitum***. SYSTAT's limit of 256 variables applies to **MACRO** as well.

Line numbers

Macros do not need line numbers unless the %GOTO command and/or **MACRO** text lines are used, or if they are submitted from other procedures.

All line numbers must be positive integers.

If a macro has line numbers then each line, including subroutines, ***must*** have a unique line number. **MACRO** does not warn you if it encounters duplicate or out-of-sequence line numbers.

If one macro %LOADs another, it does not matter if they share line numbers. The %LOAD command clears current line numbers before loading and executing the new macro.

MACRO BASIC programs must be numbered if they are submitted from another SYSTAT procedure.

Only numbered **MACRO** BASIC lines can be LISTed or modified. We recommend that you number all of your **MACRO** BASIC programs.

Invoking DOS commands

Changing drives or directories from within **MACRO** is difficult for SYSTAT to process and may cause your system to crash.

Recursive subroutines

MACRO's subroutines support recursion. In other words, a subroutine can call itself. **MACRO**'s recursion, however, differs from traditional recursion found in languages such as PASCAL or BASIC in the following ways:

1) Local variables are not supported.
2) The available "subroutine stack" is not influenced by the number of variables in the macro, but rather by how deep the subroutine is "nested" (i.e. how many times it has successively called itself).

The RUN Command

SYSTAT does not clear the workspace after it executes a macro. The last value calculated for each variable remains in memory and the random number seed is not reinitialized.

Advanced topics in MACRO

This section includes examples that demonstrate the more advanced features of **MACRO**. We will discuss subroutines, looping structures, user-geared menu generation, and string manipulation. Many of these examples include **DATA** commands that perform the same function.

11.18 Using a SYSTAT file of unknown length

The example below shows the simplest way to read data from a data file of unknown length and save that data to another data file. EOF is a built-in variable that is false for each case except the last:

MACRO

```
USE SYS1
SAVE SYS2
10 %READ
20 %WRITE
30 %IF EOF THEN %GOTO 50
40 %GOTO 10
50 %STOP
RUN
```

DATA

```
USE SYS1
SAVE SYS2
RUN
```

11.18 Using a %FOR... %NEXT loop with a file of unknown length

This example uses the %FOR...%NEXT loop without specifying the number of cases in the SYSTAT file SYS1. This does not work with more than 32,000 cases.

MACRO

```
USE SYS1
SAVE SYS2
10 %LET MAXCASE = 32000
20 %FOR I = 1 TO MAXCASE
30   %READ
40   %WRITE
50   %IF EOF THEN %GOTO 70
60 %NEXT
70 %STOP
DROP MAXCASE
RUN
```

DATA

```
USE SYS1
SAVE SYS2
RUN
```

11.20 Lagging variables

This example creates a lag variable. A lag is a copy of a variable offset by a number of cases. Lags are used in time series and forecasting to see if a variable is auto- or self-correlated. The example is done in two parts. The first creates a variable X, and the second creates a variable LAG1 which is a lag of X:

MACRO	*DATA*
`SAVE FILE1`	`SAVE FILE1`
`%FOR I = 1 TO 5`	`REPEAT 5`
`  %LET X = I`	`LET X = CASE`
`  %WRITE`	`RUN`
`%NEXT`	
`RUN`	
`NEW`	
`USE FILE1`	`USE FILE1`
`SAVE FILE2`	`SAVE FILE2`
`%LET LAG1 = .`	`HOLD`
`%FOR I = 1 TO 5`	`IF BOF THEN LET LAG0 = .`
`  %READ`	
`  %WRITE`	`LET LAG1 = LAG0`
`  %LET LAG1 = X`	`LET LAG0 = X`
`%NEXT`	`DROP LAG0`
`RUN`	`RUN`
`NEW`	

Notice that **MACRO** does not need the HOLD command to lag variables. The ability to use the %FOR...%NEXT loop across cases allows a great degree of flexibility. In this example the first case is a missing value for the variable LAG1. Here is what is in FILE2 after either of the above programs are executed:

CASE	X	LAG1
1	1	.
2	2	1
3	3	2
4	4	3
5	5	4

11.21 Summing across cases

This example sums variables across cases. The method is similar to that for lagging variables. Again the HOLD command is not needed in the **MACRO**. The new variable SUM is set to 0 in **DATA** because HOLD initializes all new variables to 0. In **MACRO**, however, SUM has to be assigned the value of 0.

MACRO

```
SAVE FILE1
%FOR I = 1 TO 5
  %LET X = %ZRN
  %WRITE
%NEXT
RUN
NEW
```

DATA

```
SAVE FILE1
REPEAT 5
LET X = ZRN
RUN
```

```
USE FILE1
SAVE FILE2
%LET SUM = 0
%FOR I = 1 TO 5
  %READ
  %LET SUM = SUM + X
  %WRITE
%NEXT
RUN
NEW
```

```
USE FILE1
SAVE FILE2
HOLD
LET SUM = SUM + X
RUN
```

Since **MACRO** and **DATA** have the same default random number seeds, the two programs create identical SYSTAT files. Here is what is in FILE2 after either program executes:

CASE	X	SUM
1	0.071	0.071
2	0.355	0.426
3	-0.176	0.251
4	-0.043	0.208
5	1.572	1.780

11.22 Nesting %FOR... %NEXT loops

A useful feature of **MACRO** is its ability to nest %FOR...%NEXT loops:

```
SAVE DATAFILE
%DIM A(5)
%FOR I = 1 TO 10
  %CALL GETDATA
  %WRITE
  %NEXT
%STOP

%SUB GETDATA
%FOR J = 1 TO 5
  %LET NUM = J
  %PROMPT 'ENTER VARIABLE # &NUM: '
  %INPUT A(J)
%NEXT
%ENDSUB
```

The example above shows how you may call a subroutine that has a %FOR...%NEXT loop from within a %FOR...%NEXT loop. This program reads values for subscripted variables A(1) thru A(5), writes the case to a SYSTAT file, and repeats the process ten times.

Loops *cannot* be directly nested, e.g.:

```
%FOR I = 1 to 10
  %FOR J = 1 to 5
  macro commands
  %NEXT
%NEXT
```

is incorrect.

11.23 Chaining macros

This example shows how to chain macros together. The %LOAD command executes a tokenized macro. Notice that %LOAD automatically clears any instructions in memory, reads the macro to be loaded, and executes the new instructions. Control does *not* automatically return to the original macro when the second macro finishes executing.

```
10 %PRINT 'IN FIRST MACRO'
20 %PROMPT 'MORE?'
30 %INPUT X$
40 %IF X$='N' OR X$='n' THEN %GOTO 100
50 %LOAD MACRO2
100 STOP
STORE MACRO1
NEW

10 %PRINT 'IN SECOND MACRO'
20 %LOAD MACRO1
STORE MACRO2
NEW

LOAD MACRO1
RUN
```

The output is:

```
IN FIRST MACRO
IN SECOND MACRO
```

11.24 Recursive subroutines (subroutines that CALL themselves)

This procedure prompts the user to enter a number. If the value entered is illegal (e.g., the character a) the program prompts the user for another value. This process repeats indefinitely until the user enters a valid number.

```
%CALL INPUTNUM
%PRINT 'NUMBER IS: &NUMBER'

%SUB INPUTNUM
%PROMPT 'ENTER ANY NUMBER: '
%INPUT NUMBER
%IF NUMBER = . THEN %CALL INPUTNUM
%ENDSUB
```

A subroutine can call itself 400 times consecutively before **MACRO** runs out of memory.

11.25 Creating SYSTAT command files with macros

This example shows a macro that prompts the user for information and saves that information into a command file. The user can then submit the command file (in this case, COMMAND.CMD) to the appropriate SYSTAT procedure. Here, the resulting command file lists a specified number of cases from a selected data file:

```
FORMAT 0
10 %CLEAR
20 %PROMPT 'This macro creates a command file'
30 %PROMPT 'that will go to DATA
40 %PROMPT 'and list cases from a file..'
70 %PROMPT 'ENTER FILE NAME TO LIST:'
80 %INPUT FILENAME$
90 %PROMPT 'ENTER NUMBER OF CASES TO LIST:'
100 %INPUT NUMCASE
110 %OUTPUT 'COMMAND.CMD'
120 USE &FILENAME$
130 REPEAT &NUMCASE
140 CASELIST
150 RUN
160           (line intentionally left blank)
170 %OUTPUT *
180 %SWITCHTO DATA 'COMMAND.CMD'
```

If MYFILE is entered as the file name and 10 as the number of cases, then the file COMMAND.CMD has the following lines:

```
USE MYFILE
REPEAT 10
CASELIST
RUN
```

The command FORMAT = 0 is included so that the number after the REPEAT command is an integer. The blank line provides a carriage return when SYSTAT asks the user to confirm that data is not to be saved to a SYSTAT file.

You can prompt the user to identify the variables to list by making a few changes to the macro above, as follows:

```
FORMAT 0
 10 %CLEAR
 20 %PROMPT 'ENTER FILE NAME TO LIST:'
 30 %INPUT FILENAME$
 40 %PROMPT 'ENTER # OF CASES TO LIST:'
 50 %INPUT NUMCASE
 60 %OUTPUT COMMAND
 70 USE &FILENAME$
 80 REPEAT &NUMCASE
 90 %CALL GETNAMES
100 CASELIST &VAR1$ &VAR2$ &VAR3$ &VAR4$ &VAR5$
110 RUN
130 %OUTPUT *
140 %SWITCHTO DATA 'COMMAND.DAT'

500 %SUB GETNAMES
510 %PROMPT 'ENTER VAR NAMES (5 AT MOST).'
520 %PROMPT 'PRESS ENTER WHEN FINSIHED'
530 %INPUT VAR1$  AT 4  1
540 %IF VAR1$ <> ' ' THEN %INPUT VAR2$
550 %IF VAR2$ <> ' ' THEN %INPUT VAR3$
560 %IF VAR3$ <> ' ' THEN %INPUT VAR4$
570 %IF VAR4$ <> ' ' THEN %INPUT VAR5$
580 %IF VAR5$ <> ' ' THEN %INPUT VAR6$
590 %IF VAR6$ <> ' ' THEN %INPUT VAR7$
600 %IF VAR7$ <> ' ' THEN %INPUT VAR8$
610 %ENDSUB
```

If the following line is included in the macro, the program will SWITCHTO **STATS** and execute the commands that appear in the file MORE.CMD:

```
125 %SWITCHTO STATS 'MORE.CMD'
```

11.26 Using the %MENU command

One of **MACRO**'s powerful interactive features is the %MENU command, which allows you to present the user with a menu from which s/he can choose several operations. The following example generates a three-choice main menu. The first item on this menu (DOS COMMANDS) generates a 4 choice submenu. Choice 2 in the main menu invokes a commercial DOS shell program called Norton Commander; control is passed to Norton Commander and returns to the macro only when that program is exited. You should note that, because **MACRO** is still loaded in memory while any macro is running, the memory size of any other program which may be run in this fashion is limited to approximately 170K.

```
10 %MENU CHOICE 'MAIN MENU'/'DOS COMMANDS',
     'NORTON COMMANDER','QUIT'
20 %IF CHOICE=1 THEN %CALL DOS
40 %ELSE %IF CHOICE=2 THEN %DOS 'C:\UTIL\NC'
50 %ELSE %IF CHOICE=3 THEN %STOP
60 %GOTO 10
70 %SUB DOS
80 %MENU CHOICE 'DOS MENU' / 'ERASE FILE','COPY FILE',
    'ANY COMMAND','MAIN MENU'
90 %IF CHOICE=1 THEN %CALL ERASEFIL
100 %IF CHOICE=2 THEN %CALL COPYFILE
110 %IF CHOICE=3 THEN %CALL GENERIC
120 %IF CHOICE=4 THEN %GOTO 10
130 %GOTO 80
140 %ENDSUB
150 %SUB ERASEFIL
160 %PROMPT 'ENTER FILE NAME TO ERASE:'
170 %INPUT FILE$
180 %DOS 'ERASE &FILE$'
190 %ENDSUB
200 %SUB COPYFILE
210 %PROMPT 'SOURCE FILE NAME:'
220 %INPUT FROM$
230 %PROMPT 'TARGET FILE NAME:'
240 %INPUT TO$
250 %DOS 'COPY &FROM$ &TO$'
255 %DOS 'PAUSE'
260 %ENDSUB
270 %SUB GENERIC
280 %PROMPT 'ENTER DOS COMMAND'
```

```
290 %INPUT COMMAND$
300 %PROMPT 'ENTER COMMAND PARAMETERS OR <CR> FOR NONE'
310 %INPUT PARAM$
320 %DOS '&COMMAND$ &PARAM$'
325 %DOS 'PAUSE'
330 %ENDSUB
340 %STOP
```

Note that this macro makes extensive use of subroutines and the interactive %PROMPT and %INPUT commands. It also uses the %DOS command, MACRO's equivalent to the DOS command, to pass instructions to DOS via text substitution. The PAUSE command in lines 255 and 325 tells DOS to halt processing until a key is pressed; this allows the output of the DOS command executed by the preceding DOS command to remain on screen while you view it.

Appendix I: DATA command reference

APPEND	Joins files vertically
ARRAY	Aliases variables to an array of subscripted variables
CODE	Recodes values
DELETE	Deletes current case from the file that is saved
DIAGONAL	Signals that the diagonal is missing from the triangular matrix being input
DIM	Creates new subscripted variables
DROP	Drops variable from the file that is saved
ELSE	Executes subsequent statements if the previous IF test was not met
ERASE	Erases lines from a SYSTAT BASIC program
FOR...NEXT	Begins a loop or statement group
GET	Reads data from plain text file
GOTO	Detours to a specific line in a BASIC program
HOLD	Retains values from one operation to the next
IF...THEN	Executes operation if condition is met
INPUT	Inputs text data in a fixed-format or free-format
LABEL	Creates value labels
LET	Assigns a value to a variable
LIST	Displays values of the variables you specify
NEXT	Ends a FOR...NEXT loop
PRINT	Prints variables and/or character strings
PUT	Saves data in a plain text file with comma delimiters
RANK	Replaces values in variable with ranks
REPEAT	Specifies the number of cases to process
RSEED	Sets random number seed
RUN	Runs a SYSTAT job
SORT	Sorts data
STANDARDIZE	Standardizes variables
STOP	Stops processing of a case
TRANSPOSE	Transposes a file
TYPE	Reads non-rectangular data
USE	Opens data file, or joins two files horizontally

See Chapter 6 for information on built-in functions and variables.

Eight global commands—FORMAT, HELP, NOTE, OPTIONS, PAGE, SELECT, SUBMIT, and QUIT—are discussed at the beginning of the reference.

Appendix I: DATA command reference

Overview

This appendix presents syntax information and summaries of all the **DATA** commands in alphabetical order. We identify the chapter(s) that introduce each command in the left margin.

The opposite page shows all the **DATA** commands with brief explanations.

The command reference begins with a list of common commands that are available globally—with SYSTAT, **SYGRAPH**, *and* **DATA** . They might be useful in **DATA** . These commands are also shown in the **Command reference** appendices of the *Statistics* and *Graphics* volumes.

Global commands

FORMAT=*n*	Specifies the number of decimals to display in output ($0 \leq n \leq 9$). The default is 3. COLD.
/UNDERFLOW	Prints tiny numbers that otherwise would appear as "0" in exponential notation.
HELP *command*	Displays help for specified *command.* HOT.
NOTE=*n* | '*line1*' ['*line2* ...]	Prints any note (character string) in the text output, or the printer or file if output is redirected. HOT. NOTE can print ASCII characters by their index; specify the index number without quotation marks. For instance, NOTE=13 puts a bell in the output. (You can specify both an index and a character string in a single line.) HOT.
OPTIONS	Displays options currently in effect. Not available in the Data Editor. HOT.

PAGE	Selects screen display and printer output format and characteristics with the options that follow. COLD.
FILE=*n*	Specifies the number of lines per page in a text file. The default value is 56. Specify 0 for no page breaks.
PRINTER=*n*	Specifies the number of lines per printed page. The default value is 56. Specify 0 for no page breaks.
NARROW I WIDE	Specifies the number of columns used for analysis (text) output. NARROW, the default, specifies 80 columns; WIDE specifies 132.
TITLE='*line1*', '*line2*', ...	Specifies a title for each page of output. You may specify up to 10 title lines; each line may be up to 132 characters long. SYSTAT centers each line on the page.
SELECT *exprn1* [...]	Selects a subgroup of cases for analysis. You may include up to 10 expressions. Only cases meeting all the expression conditions are used. Using the SELECT command without an argument ends current selection conditions. COLD.
SUBMIT "*filename*"	Reads and executes commands contained in *filename*. *Filename* must be a text file. HOT.
/ECHO	Displays the commands in *filename* as they are processed.

	QUIT [= * | @ | "*filename*"	Exits SYSTAT to the Finder. The optional arguments let you output the command log to a specific destination. Asterisk (*) sends the command log to the screen only. At-sign (@) sends the command log to a printer and the screen. "*Filename*" sends the command log to the screen and a text file called *filename*. Not available in the Data Editor. HOT.
DATA commands Chapter 5	**APPEND** *file1 file2*	Creates a new file (named by a SAVE command) by appending cases of *file2* at the bottom after cases of *file1*. Both files must contain the same variables, in the same order, but they can have different numbers of cases. You must use SAVE before APPEND, which is HOT.
Chapter 10	**ARRAY** *array / varlist*	Aliases the variables in *varlist* to an array of subscripted variables. The variables have the root name *array* with integer subscripts 1 through *n*, where *n* is the number of variables in *varlist*. Note that ARRAY works differently in versions prior to 3.2.
Chapter 6	**CODE** *varlist / old1=new1, old2=new2, ..., oldp=newp*	Recodes the variables listed in *varlist*. For all the variables in *varlist*, any case with value *old1* is replaced with value *new1*. All occurrences of *old2* are replaced with *new2*, etc. All variables in *varlist* must be the same type (character or numeric), and the *oldp* and new*p* values must correspond to the variable type. Surround character strings with single or double quotation marks.
Chapter 5	**DELETE**	Prevents the current case from being written to the SAVE file. Usually, use DELETE with an IF...THEN command.

Chapter 3	<u>DIAGONAL=PRESENT</u> | ABSENT	Specifies whether the matrix you are entering has values in the diagonal cells. The diagonal is assumed to be present unless you state otherwise with DIAGONAL=ABSENT.
Chapter 7	**DIM** *var(n)*	Reserves space for a new variable *var* with subscript *n*, where *n* is an integer between 1 and 99 inclusive.
Chapter 5	**DROP** *varlist*	Prevents the variables given by *varlist* from being written to the file named by SAVE.
Chapter 7	**ELSE** *statement*	Can follow an IF...THEN command. *Statement* is executed when the IF *exprn* evaluates as false. The *statement* can be any valid command, including DELETE or another IF...THEN command.
Chapter 7	**ERASE** *n1*[–*n2*]	Erases all numbered BASIC statements from *n1* to *n2*, inclusive, or erases the line numbered *n1*, if a single number (rather than a range) is specified. The default, if no range is specified, is all numbered statements.
Chapter 7	**FOR** [*index=n1* **TO** *n2* [**STEP=***n3*]] ... **NEXT**	Starts a FOR...NEXT loop. *Index* must be a numeric variable, either from your file or a new variable. You must specify *n1*, but *n2* is optional. You may optionally specify an increment value with the STEP=*n3* phrase; the default is +1. You may specify any real number for *n1–3*. See text for instructions on using FOR...NEXT with an without an *index*.
Chapter 3	**GET** *filename*	Reads the ASCII (plain text) file *filename*.

Chapter 7	**GOTO** *n*	Detours the program to the statement numbered *n*. You must have numbered line statements in your program to use GOTO.
Chapter 10	**HOLD**	Initializes all numeric values in a BASIC program to zero and retains numeric values from one case to the next. HOLD stays in effect until you QUIT the program, type NEW, or USE another file.
Chapters 6, 7	**IF** *exprn* **THEN** *statement*	Executes *statement* if the *exprn* evaluates as true. *Exprn* may be any valid expression formed with numbers, variables, operators, and functions. *Statement* may be any valid command, including DELETE. You can follow IF...THEN constructions with ELSE (see).
Chapter 3	**INPUT** *varlist*	Names the variables (and indicates order) that will be read into SYSTAT. You may identify a range of variables in *varlist* using subscript notation. For fixed-format input, INPUT has two arguments, each enclosed in parentheses: INPUT (*varlist*) (*format*). As above, *varlist* indicates the variable names, in order. *Format* is a format description in special notation, discussed in this chapter. For free-format input (first syntax above), place a backslash after *varlist* to force SYSTAT to start a new case for each line of data and to use every value entered in each row, even if it must start filling new cases to do so. See Example 3.8.

Chapter 6	**LABEL** *varlist* / *old1=label1, old2=label2, ..., oldp=labelp*	Creates a character variable for each numeric variable in *varlist*. *Varlist* can contain numeric variables only. For each numeric variable, a character variable with the same name plus $ is created, with values as given by *oldi=labeli*. If any character variable already exists, its values are replaced.
Chapter 6	**LET** *var=exprn*	Assigns the value of *exprn* to the variable *var*. You may use either a numeric or character variable. Character values must be surrounded by single or double quotation marks.
Chapter 2	**LIST** [*varlist*]	Lists the contents of the file named by the USE statement. *Varlist* is an optional list of variables for viewing only a portion of the file.
Chapter 2	**LRECL=***n*	Specifies record length for importing data. *N* is an integer between 0 and 999. You must use LRECL if you are importing data from record longer than 150 columns.
Chapter 7	**NEXT**	Ends a FOR...NEXT (see) loop.
Chapters 2, 7	**PRINT** *varlist* | '*string*'	Displays the values of the variables listed in *varlist*, or displays the character *string* you specify. *Varlist* may include numeric or character variables.
Chapter 4	**PUT** *filename*	Saves data in a SYSTAT data file into a plain text (ASCII) file.

Chapter 8	**RANK** *varlist*	Transforms all numeric variables in *varlist* to ranks. Each variable is ranked within its own distribution. The default is all numeric variables in the file.
Chapters 2, 7	**REPEAT** *n*	Applies subsequent commands to the first *n* cases in the file.
Chapter 10	**RSEED=***n*	Specifies the random number seed *n*. The default is 313. You can specify any integer between 1 and 30,000.
Chapter 2	**RUN**	Sets a **DATA** procedure in motion. HOT.
Chapter 8	**SORT** *varlist*	Sorts the datafile on the variables specified in *varlist. Varlist* can include numeric or character variables or both. The default is all variables in the file, in the order that they appear in the file.
Chapter 8	**STANDARDIZE** *varlist*	Standardizes the numeric variables named in *varlist.* The default is all numeric variables in the file.
Chapter 7	**STOP**	Stops execution of a BASIC program.
Chapter 5	**TRANSPOSE**	Transposes a data file by turning rows (cases) into columns (variables) and vice versa. You can only transpose files with numeric data. TRANSPOSE can handle a maximum of 99 cases (before transposing).

Chapter 3	**TYPE =** RECTANGULAR | SSCP | COVARIANCE | CORRELATION | DISSIMILARITY | SIMILARITY	Specifies the type of matrix you are entering. Use DIAGONAL=ABSENT if the diagonal values are missing.
Chapters 2, 5	**USE** *filename* [(*varlist*)]	Retrieves the file *filename*. If you include the optional *varlist*, USE retrieves only the specified variables from the SYSTAT file *filename*.
	USE *file1* [(*varlist*)] *file2* [(*varlist*)]	Brings both *file1* and *file2* into the active workspace. You can merge these files into a single third file. Use the optional *varlists* if you want to merge only portions of the file(s).

Appendix II: MACRO command reference

BY	Activates the BOG and EOG variables
DROP	Drops variable from the file that is saved
ERASE	Erases lines from a **MACRO** BASIC program
LIST	Lists current macro lines to output device
LOAD	Retrieves a binary copy of macro
NEW	Clears workspace
RUN	Executes macro
SAVE	Saves data to specified file
STORE	Writes binary copy of a macro to disk
%CALL	Transfers program control to a subroutine
%CHR	Returns ASCII character corresponding to a specified number
%CLEAR	Clears the screen
%DIM	Creates new subscripted variables
%DOS	Executes a DOS command from within **MACRO**
%EDIT	Performs special format conversion
%ELSE	Executes subsequent statements if the previous %IF test was not met
%ENDSUB	Ends definition of a subroutine
%FOR	Starts a %FOR...%NEXT loop
%GOTO	Passes program control to a specified line
%IF...THEN	Executes operation if condition is met
%INDEX	Returns the position of a string in a character variable
%INPUT	Reads the value of a variable entered from keyboard
%LET	Assigns a value to a variable
%LOAD	Loads and executes a macro
%MENU	Writes a menu to the screen
%NEXT	Ends a %FOR...%NEXT loop
%OUTPUT	Redirects output to specified device
%PRINT	Prints to output device
%PRINTNOLF	Prints without a linefeed
%PROMPT	Prints to screen
%READ	Reads one record of data from current file
%STOP	Stops execution of macro
%SUB	Begins definition of subroutine
%SUBSTR	Returns a portion of a character variable
%SWITCHTO	Switches to another SYSTAT procedure
%WRITE	Writes a case to the current SAVE file

Appendix II: MACRO command reference

Overview

This appendix presents syntax information and summaries of all the **MACRO** commands. We first list *command level commands*. These commands are not BASIC commands but may be used in **MACRO** programs. Next, we list *MACRO BASIC commands*. Finally we list *character functions*, which are used for string manipulation.

The opposite page shows all the **MACRO** commands with brief explanations.

For information about the syntax used in this reference, see the **Command reference** in the *Statistics* or *Graphics* volumes.

MACRO Command level commands	**BY** *varlist*	Activates the two system variables BOG (beginning of group) and EOG (end of group).
	DROP *varlist*	Prevents the variables in *varlist* from being written to your SAVE file. You must include a varlist.
	ERASE *line1–line2*	Erases all numbered BASIC statements from *line1* to *line2*. The default is all numbered BASIC statements.
	LIST *line1–line2*	Prints the current **MACRO** BASIC lines to the output device. The default is all lines.
	LOAD *macroname*	Retrieves a binary copy of the macro program *macroname*.
	NEW	Clears the entire workspace. All open files are closed and all commands are erased from memory.
	RUN	Begins execution of your **MACRO** BASIC program. HOT.
	SAVE *filename*	Saves your data into the SYSTAT file *filename*. You must enter SAVE before RUN to create a SYSTAT file.
	/ 'comment'	Saves your comment to the SYSTAT file.
	<u>DOUBLE</u> | SINGLE	Writes in double or single precision.

	STORE *filename*	Writes a binary copy of a **MACRO** program to disk. The default extension is .TOK.
MACRO BASIC commands	%**CALL** *subname*	Transfers control to the **MACRO** subroutine *subname.*
	%**CLEAR**	Clears the screen.
	%**DIM** *dimvar [n]*	Declares and dimensions the subscripted variable *dimvar. Dimvar* must be a numeric variable. *N* is the number of levels for *dimvar* and must be an integer between 1 and 99.
	%**DOS** *'command'*	Executes the DOS command from within a running macro.
	%**ELSE** *statement*	Executes the following statement if the preceding statement is false.
	%**ENDSUB**	Ends the definition of a **MACRO** subroutine.
	%**FOR** *indexvar=n1* **TO** *n2* **STEP=***stepnum*	Starts a FOR-NEXT loop. *Indexvar* must be a numeric variable. *Indexvar* is only saved to your file if it appears in your USEd file or you use it as something other than an index variable. You must specify *n1. N2* is optional. The default *stepnum* is +1. You can specify any real number for any of these parameters.

%**GOTO** *linenum*	Passes program control to the BASIC line *linenum.* You must have line numbers in your program to use GOTO. You must specify a value for *linenum.*
%**IF** *statement*	Continues program flow if statement is true.
%**INPUT** *varname* **AT** *row col*	Reads the value of a variable from the keyboard. It optionally moves the cursor to a specified row *(row)* and column *(col)* on the screen before reading the value. The default row and column is the current cursor position.
%**INSERT** *filename*	Reads ASCII text from an existing file and writes it to the output device.
/ START='string'	Includes text following the first occurrence of *string.*
END='string'	Concludes insertion of text at the first occurrence of *string.*
%**LET** *var=value*	Assigns the variable *var* the value of *value.*
%**LOAD** *filename*	Loads and executes the macro program *filename.* The default extension for *filename* is .TOK. The default location is the current drive and subdirectory.
%**MENU** *menuvar 'title'/ 'choice1', 'choice2',... 'choicep'*	Writes a menu to the screen and returns the choice entered by the user. *Menuvar* is the numeric variable that holds the menu choice. *Title* is the menu title. You can identify as many as 20 menu choices. A single menu choice cannot be broken across multiple lines.

%NEXT	Ends a %FOR–%NEXT loop.
%OUTPUT	Redirects output to the output device. Output is always echoed to the screen.
= * | @ | *filename*	* redirects output to the screen. @ directs output to the printer. *Filename* sends output to the file *filename.* The default extension of *filename* is .DAT. The default location is the current drive and subdirectory.
%PRINT *stuff2print*	Prints *stuff2print* to the output device. *Stuff2print* can include variables, string expressions, and/or the CHR function.
%PRINTNOLF *stuff2print*	Prints *stuff2print* to the printer without a linefeed. *Stuff2print* can include variables, string expressions, and/or the CHR function.
%PROMPT *stuff2prompt*	Prints *stuff2prompt* to the screen. *Stuff2prompt* can include variables, string expressions, and/or the CHR function.
%READ	Reads one record of data from the current USE file.
%STOP	Stops execution of a BASIC program.
%SUB *subname*	Begins definition of the **MACRO** subroutine *subname.*

	%SWITCHTO *module batchfile*	Exits **MACRO** and enters the SYSTAT module *module.* You must specify a file of SYSTAT commands (*batchfile)*. When the processing of *batchfile* is complete, SYSTAT returns to **MACRO**.
	/ ECHO	Prints the commands in *batchfile* to the screen as they are being processed.
	%WRITE	Writes all active variables to the SYSTAT file specified with the SAVE command. Active variables are the variables in a USEd file or variables declared in the **MACRO** program, and variables that have not been DROPped.
Character functions	**%CHR** *(asciinum)*	Returns the ASCII character corresponding to *asciinum. Asciinum* can range from 0 to 255. You can only use this function in conjunction with the %LET command.
	%EDIT *(var$; format)*	Performs special format conversion. You can only use this function in conjunction with the %LET command. Valid formats ar DOLLAR, COMMA, YYDDD, POUND,YEN, SSN, NUMBER, and numeric formats (e.g., #12.2)
	%INDEX *(var$; 'string')*	Returns the location of *string* in the character variable *var$*. You can only use this function in conjunction with the %LET command.
	%SUBSTR*(source$; location; numchar)*	Returns a subset of characters from the character variable *source$*. You can only use this function in conjunction with the %LET command.

Appendix III: SYSTAT file structure

SYSTAT data files have a simple structure. Data are stored in cases by variables format, with each case written as a single unformatted FORTRAN record. Triangular matrices are stored in the same form (i.e. as many cases as variables) with entries above the diagonal replaced by missing values.

Records

First record

The first record contains three integer variables: Version, Release, and Mod. For Version 3.0 and 4.0, these are 30, 0, and 0, respectively. Notice that NV, MTYPE, and NTYPE are used to read these variables in subroutine GETLAB below. This allows Version 2 and later to read Version 1 files.

Second record

The second and later records contain comment fields, one record per comment. These records are terminated by a record that begins with a $.

Third record

The next record contains three integer variables. NV is the number of variables in the file. MTYPE is the type of file. The values of MTYPE are:

1 Rectangular data
2 SSCP matrix
3 Covariance matrix
4 Correlation matrix
5 Dissimilarity matrix
6 Similarity matrix

You may extend these values to accommodate other types, but inform SYSTAT for compatibility.

The third variable, NTYPE, specifies the precision of the numerical data in the file. Double precision (standard) is NTYPE=2, and single precision is NTYPE=1.

The next NV records contain the variable labels in the first 12 bytes of each record. On some operating systems with 128 byte or longer records, this wastes some space, but putting labels on separate records in the file simplifies variable subsetting algorithms. Labels are right justified in the first 8 characters of the label field (i.e. leading blanks). The remaining 4 characters are reserved for subscripts.Character variable labels have no subscripts, and are identified by a $ in the 9th byte of the label. Otherwise, labels are for numerical variables. The subroutine GETLAB below reads NV, MTYPE, and NTYPE, fills the array LAB with NV labels, and records how many variables are of type numerical (ND) and character (NK).

Remaining records

The remaining records contain the data until the end of file marker. ND numerical and NK character variables are written in a single unformatted WRITE. Character variable values are stored as 12 bytes, left justified (padded on the right with blanks).

Subroutines

The subroutine GETLAB below reads the header information from the file. Once it has been called, you have the information necessary to read the records in the file with RSYS. GETLAB thus can be used to rewind a file to begin reading it again with RSYS.

The subroutine RSYS below reads a record (case) from a SYSTAT file and places the values into the same order in DAT and KHR as they are in the LAB labels array. After RSYS is called to read a record, values for a character variable in column i of the LAB array can be found in column *i* of KHR and values for a numerical variable in column *j* in the LAB array can be found in column *j* of DAT. If you are writing routines that process only numerical data, you can call RSYS and ignore KHR (although be sure to dimension it correctly in the calling routine). RSYS filters character variables out of the file by putting them in KHR.

The subroutine WSYS writes a record to a SYSTAT file. You must set ND to the number of numerical variables in LAB and NK to the number of character variables in KHR. If you have no character variables, set NK=0 and WSYS will write only numerical variables into the file. You may set ND=0 for writing only character variables.

DAT and KHR thus serve as I/O buffers whose contents correspond (column by column) with the labels in LAB. If you wish to use random access I/O, you can use WSYS to get sequential records from a SYSTAT file and save them into a direct access file with REC=N, where N is the current record number of the record just read from the SYSTAT file. Some of the SYSTAT routines do this for sorting and other tasks.

Missing data and precision

Missing data are represented by a variable DMIS, which is –1.0D36. The single precision missing data value is RMIS, which is –1.0E36. All real arithmetic is bounded by + and – OFLO, which is 1.0D35. Single precision overflow is ROFLO, which is 1.0E35. Machine precision is EPS, which is 1.0D–15. Single precision machine precision is REPS, which is 1.0E–7. Greater precision is available on most machines, but these numbers insure common arithmetical bounds on all machines with double precision arithmetic. SYSTAT prints a maximum of 12 digits, so there is always at least (usually more) 3 digits of fuzz to allow for round-off errors. On MS-DOS machines, all INTEGER variables in these 3 subroutines are INTEGER*2. On other machines, they are INTEGER*4.

```
C***********************************************************************
      SUBROUTINE GETLAB (LAB,MTYPE,NTYPE,KU,EOF,ND,NK,NV,MV)
C
C GET SYSTAT FILE HEADER INFO
C
C      YOU MUST PREVIOUSLY HAVE OPENED FILE TO READ WITH:
C
C      OPEN (KU,FILE=name,STATUS='OLD',FORM='UNFORMATTED')
C
C LAB = VARIABLE LABEL ARRAY
C MTYPE = TYPE OF FILE (1=RECT,2=SSCP,3=COVA,4=CORR,5=SIMI,6=DISS)
C NTYPE = NUMERICAL DATA TYPE (1=SINGLE PRECISION,2=DOUBLE PRECISION)
C KU = INPUT UNIT NUMBER
C EOF = END OF FILE
C ND = NUMBER OF DATA ITEMS (NUMERIC VARIABLES) IN RECORD
C NK = NUMBER OF CHARACTER ITEMS (CHARACTER VARIABLES) IN RECORD
C NV = ND+NK  (TOTAL NUMBER OF VARIABLES PER CASE)
C MV = MAXIMUM NUMBER OF VARIABLES IN FILE
C
C NV IS USED IN FIRST READ TO REPRESENT VERSION
C MTYPE IS USED IN FIRST READ TO REPRESENT RELEASE
C IF NTYPE IS NEGATIVE IN FIRST READ, VERSION .GE. 2
C
      LOGICAL EOF
      CHARACTER*1 LAB
C IF MS-DOS OR CP/M UNCOMMENT FOLLOWING LINE
C      INTEGER*2 KVER,KREL,KMOD
      DIMENSION LAB(12,MV)
C
      COMMON /VERSN/ KVER,KREL,KMOD
C
      EOF=.TRUE.
      REWIND KU
      READ (KU,END=100,ERR=100) NV,MTYPE,NTYPE
      IF (NTYPE.GT.KMOD) GO TO 5
      IF (NV+MTYPE.GT.KVER+KREL) GO TO 100
    1 READ (KU,END=100,ERR=100) ((LAB(I,J),I=1,12),J=1,6)
      IF (LAB(1,1).NE.'$') GO TO 1
      DO 3 I=1,12
         DO 2 J=1,MV
            LAB(I,J)=' '
    2    CONTINUE
    3 CONTINUE
      READ (KU,END=100,ERR=100) NV,MTYPE,NTYPE
    5 ND=0
      NK=0
      DO 10 J=1,NV
         READ (KU,END=100,ERR=100) (LAB(I,J),I=1,12)
         IF (LAB(9,J).NE.'$') ND=ND+1
         IF (LAB(9,J).EQ.'$') NK=NK+1
   10 CONTINUE
      EOF=.FALSE.
  100 RETURN
      END
```

```
C***********************************************************************
      SUBROUTINE RSYS (LAB,KHR,STA,DTA,NTYPE,KU,EOF,ND,NK,MV)
C
C READ SYSTAT FILE RECORD
C
C LAB = VARIABLE LABEL ARRAY
C KHR = CHARACTER DATA ARRAY
C STA = SINGLE PRECISION DATA ARRAY
C DTA = DOUBLE PRECISION DATA (EQUIVALENCE TO STA IN CALLING ROUTINE)
C NTYPE = NUMERICAL DATA TYPE (1=SINGLE, 2=DOUBLE)
C KU = INPUT UNIT NUMBER
C EOF = END OF FILE
C ND = NUMBER OF DATA ITEMS IN RECORD
C NK = NUMBER OF CHARACTER ITEMS IN RECORD
C MV = MAXIMUM NUMBER OF VARIABLES IN FILE
C
      DOUBLE PRECISION DMIS
      DOUBLE PRECISION DTA
      LOGICAL EOF
      CHARACTER*1 LAB,KHR
C
      DIMENSION LAB(12,MV),KHR(12,MV),STA(MV),DTA(MV)
C
      RMIS=-1.0E36
      DMIS=-1.0D36
      NV=ND+NK
      EOF=.TRUE.
      IF (ND.EQ.0) GO TO 6
      IF (NTYPE.EQ.2) GO TO 5
C SINGLE PRECISION FILE DATA
      IF (NK.GT.0) READ (KU,END=100,ERR=100) (STA(J),J=1,ND),
     *                                       ((KHR(I,J),I=1,12),J=1,NK)
      IF (NK.EQ.0) READ (KU,END=100,ERR=100) (STA(J),J=1,ND)
      DO 4 I=1,ND
         IM=ND-I+1
         IF (STA(IM).NE.RMIS) DTA(IM)=STA(IM)
         IF (STA(IM).EQ.RMIS) DTA(IM)=DMIS
    4 CONTINUE
      GO TO 7
C DOUBLE PRECISION FILE DATA
    5 IF (NK.GT.0) READ (KU,END=100,ERR=100) (DTA(J),J=1,ND),
     *                                       ((KHR(I,J),I=1,12),J=1,NK)
      IF (NK.EQ.0) READ (KU,END=100,ERR=100) (DTA(J),J=1,ND)
      GO TO 7
C CHARACTER DATA ONLY IN FILE
    6 READ (KU,END=100,ERR=100) ((KHR(I,J),I=1,12),J=1,NK)
      GO TO 90
C UNPACK
    7 IF (NK.EQ.0) GO TO 90
      NDD=ND+1
      NKK=NK+1
      DO 20 J=1,NV
         JM=NV-J+1
         IF (LAB(9,JM).EQ.'$') GO TO 10
         NDD=NDD-1
         DTA(JM)=DTA(NDD)
         GO TO 20
   10    NKK=NKK-1
         DO 15 M=1,12
            KHR(M,JM)=KHR(M,NKK)
   15    CONTINUE
   20 CONTINUE
   90 EOF=.FALSE.
```



```
  100 RETURN
      END

C*********************************************************************
      SUBROUTINE WSYS (LAB,KHR,STA,DTA,NTYPE,KU,ND,NK,MV)
C
C WRITE SYSTAT FILE RECORD (DATA MUST BE IN DTA)
C
C LAB = VARIABLE LABEL ARRAY
C KHR = CHARACTER DATA ARRAY
C STA = SINGLE PRECISION DATA ARRAY
C DTA = DOUBLE PRECISION DATA (EQUIVALENCE TO STA IN CALLING ROUTINE)
C NTYPE = NUMERIC DATA TYPE (1=SINGLE, 2=DOUBLE)
C KU = OUTPUT UNIT NUMBER
C ND = NUMBER OF DATA ITEMS IN RECORD
C NK = NUMBER OF CHARACTER ITEMS IN RECORD
C MV = MAXIMUM NUMBER OF VARIABLES IN FILE
C
      DOUBLE PRECISION DMIS
      DOUBLE PRECISION DTA
      CHARACTER*1 LAB,KHR
C
      DIMENSION LAB(12,MV),KHR(12,MV),STA(MV),DTA(MV)
C
      RMIS=-1.0E36
      DMIS=-1.0D36
      NV=ND+NK
      IF (ND.EQ.0) GO TO 95
      IF (NK.EQ.0) GO TO 30
      NDD=0
      NKK=0
C PACK
      DO 20 J=1,NV
         IF (LAB(9,J).EQ.'$') GO TO 10
         NDD=NDD+1
         DTA(NDD)=DTA(J)
         GO TO 20
   10    NKK=NKK+1
         DO 15 M=1,12
            KHR(M,NKK)=KHR(M,J)
   15    CONTINUE
   20 CONTINUE
   30 IF (NTYPE.EQ.2) GO TO 90
C SINGLE PRECISION OUTPUT
      DO 85 J=1,ND
         IF (DTA(J).NE.DMIS) STA(J)=DTA(J)
         IF (DTA(J).EQ.DMIS) STA(J)=RMIS
   85 CONTINUE
      IF (NK.GT.0) WRITE (KU,ERR=100) (STA(J),J=1,ND),
     *                                ((KHR(I,J),I=1,12),J=1,NK)
      IF (NK.EQ.0) WRITE (KU,ERR=100) (STA(J),J=1,ND)
      GO TO 100
C DOUBLE PRECISION OUTPUT
   90 IF (NK.GT.0) WRITE (KU,ERR=100) (DTA(J),J=1,ND),
     *                                ((KHR(I,J),I=1,12),J=1,NK)
      IF (NK.EQ.0) WRITE (KU,ERR=100) (DTA(J),J=1,ND)
      GO TO 100
C CHARACTER OUTPUT ONLY
   95 IF (NK.GT.0) WRITE (KU,ERR=100) ((KHR(I,J),I=1,12),J=1,NK)
  100 RETURN
      END
```

Index